RELATIONSHIP REALITIES

by

Gary Freitas

Robert D. Reed Publishers • San Francisco, California

Robert D. Reed Publishers
750 La Playa Street, Suite 647
San Francisco, CA 94121
Phone: 650-994-6570 • Fax: -6579
Email: 4bobreed@msn.com
Web site: www.rdrpublishers.com

Book cover by: Julia A. Gaskill

Typesetting and Editing by: Pat Jason

Editorial Assistance by: Mark Dagger

ISBN 1-885003-71-4

Library of Congress Catalogue Number: 00-109043

Manufactured, Typeset, and Printed in
the United States of America

This book would not have been written without the inspiration of many good women and the insight, humor and compassion of some really BAD Dudes (Art, Rob, Patrick and Michel). It took a lot of beer, a lot of partying and a lot of sitting around late at night trying to make sense of it all—giving up and going home—thankful for the friendships.

Disclaimer

This book is sold with the understanding that the subject matter covered herein is of a general (and humorous) nature and does not constitute professional advice for any specific individual or situation. Readers planning to take action in any of the areas that this book describes should seek professional advice (or therapy) from their own counselors, attorneys, agents, or other advisers—as would be prudent and advisable under their given circumstances.

Contents

Are You A "BAD Dude"?

She was a comely young woman and not without prospects. Therefore it was heartbreaking to her mother that she would enter into marriage with . . . a known thief and murderer, a man of notoriously vicious and intemperate disposition.

— Unforgiven (1992 film)

This book is for men who have recently discovered that they are "BAD." For anyone who has been antisocial for a long time, don't contact us to claim: "I didn't do it!" This book is not an avenue of forgiveness. Here "BAD" refers to any guy born since the Paleolithic era, when the bad boys of patriarchy allegedly trampled the matriarchal-goddess-fallopian-utopia . . . probably while on spring break.

Definition of "BAD"

Any testosterone-enhanced Homo sapien with XY chromosome configuration and external gonad formation, who is driven by resource acquisition (money, power, toys, etc.) and dual-mating strategies (attracted to more than one woman in his lifetime)—you know, you and the posse you hang with.

If you have any doubt as to whether or not you are BAD take the test on the following page. If you answer in the affirmative to any of these statements you are politically incorrect and one BAD Dude.

1

BAD Dude Test

You . . .

__ have stopped asking, "What do women want?"

__ had to get married to find out you have a problem communicating.

__ don't believe male sexuality is the ideological equivalent of rape, in every instance.

__ find being blamed for everything wrong on the planet is starting to get to you.

__ may be biologically inferior but evolutionarily dysfunctional too!

__ haven't been completely convinced that children don't need fathers.

__ wonder if you really are responsible for the collective and brutal subjugation of women as a social class.

__ didn't know that arguments you have with your wife/girlfriend are a power struggle for "intra-species superiority."

__ fear being charged at future Nuremberg trials of being a "good husband," as part of state sanctioned human rights violation known as marriage.

__ are terrified that you will have to pay war reparations to your wife as a "Domestic Incarceration Survivor," in addition to spousal and child support.

Other contemporary books on relationships will tell you what is wrong with you as a man, and how you need to change. They will try to teach you how to become a new or improved man—more like a woman's girlfriend, or, worse, someone they think women will admire and appreciate. Trust us, they won't succeed. If you attempt to undergo gender cleansing in order to please a woman, you will fail—leading to an escalation of words and conflict as the woman in your life undergoes heterogender panic—the fear that you are no longer a *real* man.

Attitude Adjuster: *It is far more important that women deal with their dissatisfaction with men, than that men undergo change.*

This book can't help a BAD Dude get a date, get laid or even get married. But neither can any other book. What this book does offer you is the only thing you need—the right attitude. The truth is, none of the above ideological considerations have anything to do with whether or not you have a relationship—you don't need to make any deep soul-searching changes, waste your money on long-term psychotherapy or sensitivity training. Leave your "Inner Child" and "Wild Man" alone. There is no infomercial or PBS special that will make a difference in your relationship with women anyway.

You need to be informed about the rules of the game and how to play. What this book offers you is "relationship smarts," rather than the politically correct orthodoxy of learning how to communicate with women. Trying to teach men to communicate better with women, as a solution to the gender struggles of the 21st century, is like hiring more ambulance drivers to cure cancer. It's not the solution and doesn't have a clue about the problem.

3

This book explores with you the many illusions desperately deployed by both men and women in relationships (heck, maybe even by someone you know!), no matter how destructive and unworkable they have become. There are no "oughts" or "shoulds" here; no instructions or check lists. Rather than engaging in the neurotic examination of relationships and how to improve them or, worse yet, yourself, we will examine the rules of relationships and the choices before us.

Attitude Adjuster: *The first truth you must grasp is that you already have the relationship or lack of relationship you deserve.*

The illusion that this isn't true and many other self-deceptions we create are examined through a "systems approach," a methodology that informs the masculine assumptive world, along with its theorems, experimental conditions, tenets, rules, syndromes, conditions, and dick jokes that govern the orderly world as we have come to understand it.

The basic assumptions that form this book came to the BAD Dudes in five mystical revelations—during a male spiritual quest. The rest of this book came from kickin' it with a bunch of homies pissin' and moanin' about the pathetic state of our relationships with women. Be warned, this is not one of those lite-beer books that wants to make everyone feel better.

BAD Dudes—Profile In Courage

- You frequently use words such as: wimp, geek, gomer, dork, spaz, wuss, dufus, retard, dip-shit and punk ass bitch to help Dudes develop self-esteem.
- You know how to score amino acids, methamphetamines, anabolic steroid and human growth hormones at any local mini mart.
- You've been beaten and raped by women and enjoyed it.
- Your friends have learned to subdue your "roid rages" with any available 2 x 4.
- You are able to express yourself through *unsanctioned noises*—spit, fart, belch, snort, slam and break.
- You know how to take control of the TV remote, talk tech, talk sex, talk back, interrupt and dominate conversations.
- You bring a "total load" to your relationship.
- You know deep down that plaid and flannel turn a woman on.
- You tell dirty jokes and talk about your dick in the third person.
- You wake up at night to investigate psychopathic killers breaking into your home.
- You understand the intricacies of WD-40 and duct tape.
- You've mastered special communications skills to explain to a woman that tampons cause toilets to backup and overflow.
- You like to rent satanic-demon-possessed-alien-zombie-cannibalistic-stalking films and at the scariest moments grab your Old Lady's arm and shout!
- You routinely smell your pits and check your shorts for skid marks, out of respect for women.
- Your key chain is a pair of life-size, unscented, polyester blend, simulated pitbull testicles.
- When you talk affectionately about riding your hog hard, you mean your Harley, not your Old Lady.

Revelation #1:
Dating

The Subtle Perception Of The Way Things Are
(Tao-te-Ching)

Thursday night at Cow Town we got shitfaced chug-a-lugging Lone Stars and poppers, while waiting to ride the mechanical bull and trying to lick the lizard skin Tony Lamas on the hardest looking waitress we had ever seen. This impresses the women and makes your tongue feel great. However, as the only five guys in Cow Town who hugged one another and wore glasses, we immediately went from suspects to perverts because we couldn't two-step or line-dance. The waitress had us bounced when one of us stopped licking her boot and started sucking on it and got her pant leg wet.

Trying to figure out a dating relationship whose very existence is the most theoretically unstable of all possible types of relationships, is simultaneously an effort to find a stable and predictable long-term pattern in the collective feminine unconscious. It is not unlike trying to predict the weather, the stock market, or trying to have sex with every woman you're attracted to. It's not possible. So you ask yourself, how come I'm never happy with the relationship I am in? Or, why am I always sexually interested in other women—no matter how good it is with the woman I'm with currently? Is there really anyone out there who is right for me? Will I ever meet her? Will it last? Do I really want it to? Is there something wrong with me?

The subtle perception of the way things are goes beyond understanding that it is more important to wash your hands before than after going to the bathroom, or even the perception that everything is a sexual innuendo, your penis and her metaphorical one too. It is dealing with the wish, the insistence, for a mutation that reaches deep down into the recombinant processes of our DNA and makes all of this easier.

Attitude Adjuster: *You need to accept that there is nothing to be done about relationships, nothing to work on, nothing to improve. It is really very simple. There are those who are in relationships and there are those who are not. Which do you want to be? Careful, this is not a trick question.*

"Getting Over" At Nightclubs

Think "interactional synchronicity" (IS). Serious social scientists, who study the ritual of men and women picking up each other at bars and nightclubs, can provide the incorrigible a few clues that will point them in the right direction.

It should be noted that these researchers never report what type of bar tab they ran or if they picked up any women themselves as a result of their findings. In other words, did they validity-test the practical implications of their findings? In the scientific typology of desperate men, academics are right near the top.

It is not enough that they have all those young coeds running around on campus and attending their classes, they have to study women in the bars as well. They would be better off studying the more charismatic professors who are getting more nookie than they know what to do with. These gomers never understand how they could know so much and never get laid. A problem that has befuddled intellectuals for many years—trying to think their way into womans' panties. It ain't going to happen.

Phat Strategies

1st. Find A Place To Stand Without Looking Stupid. The first thing you do is establish your territory. No! You don't have to pee on anything. This is simply where you stand, preferably a spot that is not next to the speakers or too obviously in front of the women's restroom. Ideally it will be a crowded spot where women have to squeeze by you by pushing their breasts into your arms or their asses in tight skirts against your thighs. They will smile at you and you will breathe in their sweaty perfume from having just danced. You are having casual sex (frottage) with them without the formality of an introduction. Your biggest challenge will be to figure out what to do with your hands.

2nd. Attract Attention To Yourself. This is so women will notice you. This is also where the real idiots shine. Swagger about with your gut sucked in and your chest thrust out so that you "look cool, be bad." Talk loudly and ignorantly. Play air guitar and stare at womens' asses and tits as they walk by. Nudge or wink at the guy next to you, telling him to, "Go for it! She's obviously in love with you."

3rd. Primp Yourself Without Being "Totally Fabulous." Public displays of preening behavior is a primitive social cue that signals you are not just a self-absorbed and immensely insecure jerk, but also sexually available. Comb your hair and wipe the Pomade on your pant leg or restyle your mousse job; grab your crotch frequently and flash your expensive watch, diamond ear stud, gold chains, bracelets and rings. Look pissed when some guy spills his drink on your eel skin boots, but carefully wipe them off. Check to make sure your shirt collar is up at all times. However, you need to be careful about not engaging in anxious *displacement activity*. Do not pick your nose, scratch your ass, crack your knuckles, squeeze a zit, check your fly, or stupidly finish off the beer you were hoping to nurse all night. A woman would have turned away in disgust by now. You need to control this behavior.

9

4th. Give Her The "Copulatory Gaze." It's time to let her know you are a serious stud. Once you have a woman's attention you remove your sunglasses and put them on top of your head. Try to make eye contact without being caught checking out her cleavage. Keep enough distance so that she can't see your bloodshot eyes or smell your breath. A key element to mutual attraction entails a man and woman staring intently into each other's eyes for two to three seconds, then averting their eyes. (Check to see that she doesn't signal her girlfriend by putting a finger down her throat at this stage.)

5th. Smile Dorkhead. This is much harder for men, especially if they are not inebriated or joking around in the safety of friends. This takes us out of our sullen, misunderstood, "I'm-not-like-the-rest-of-the-idiots-in-here" countenance. Note if she smiles back at you, maybe opens her eyes wide, raises her eyebrows, tilts her head, then looks away. Other signals that she might be available include: if she sways her hip, arches her back, thrusts out her bosom, licks her upper lip, and/or blushes or giggles.

Okay, it's time to put up or shut up. Here is a critical juncture that the researchers never mention anything about. You have to close the distance between the two of you, whether it's a few feet or twenty yards, and then talk to her. It's almost always up to the man. You somehow have to convince her, in only a few minutes, that you are a verbal and sentient being who is visiting earth for only a short while and would she have sex or a date with you. This is where ninety percent of all attempts at picking up a woman fail. Guys never close the distance out of fear of rejection. The rest fail because they have nothing to say once they get there.

6th. Learn To Cut Your Losses. This starts with the assumption that you are already talking with a woman. The key here is to know when to cut your losses and get out before you get stupider. Once you have begun talking, you will know that she is interested if she begins to mimic your behavior and the two of you establish a common territory excluding others. This is called "interactional synchronicity" (IS)—when the two of you pivot your shoulders so that they are parallel and your bodies are face-to-face and mirroring one another. You begin to move in tandem, speak with a similar amplitude, heads bob in rhythm, arms and legs move at the same time, and you shift your weight together, etc. You both maintain deep eye contact. Advanced IS includes her rubbing her breasts against you when she is bumped, reaching out and touching you as she talks, and her asking you questions. If none of this is happenin' for you—bail now.

7th. Offer To Buy Her A Drink. Plying a woman with alcohol in an attempt to get her drunk is part of an age-old courtship strategy among primates and many other species called "courtship feeding." This impresses a woman that you are a serious hunter and gatherer and can afford to share. It will also cloud her judgment, which is to your advantage at this stage. (Warning: Do not slip "roofies" into her drink!) If you have already had too much to drink, you may find out in the morning that it was to her advantage.

Attitude Adjuster: *Now the question remains, what constitutes a successful encounter?   At one extreme is someone who won't be satisfied unless an encounter leads to a marriage in which they live together forever, until they die simultaneously.   At the other extreme is the person who feels good about himself for having tried to talk with a woman even though she wasn't interested. Did you get her real phone number, have a date, a series of dates, sex or a long term relationship? The answer is . . . it doesn't matter. You simply have to close the distance without the authorities being called.*

How To Pick Up Single Women!

√ **Does she return eye contact? No→ Terminate. Yes→Continue.** You may have to stop staring at her buff pecs and hard gluts stuffed into a tight, thong leotard!

√ **When you move closer does she move away? Yes→Terminate. No→Continue.** If your tongue is in her ear or if an appendage of yours is close to an orifice of hers, you're too close. Move back!

√ **When you speak to her does she smile and speak to you? No→Terminate. Yes→ Continue.** Does she act as if she's hearing–impaired or mute?! You should rehearse complete sentences. Don't carry on about itches, rashes or discharges.

√ **Does she help maintain the conversation? No→Terminate. Yes→Continue.** She's not asking a store manager to intervene or call 911, is she? Or does she speak in a slow, soothing voice so as not to provoke you?

√ **Are her responses yes or no, without elaboration? Yes→Terminate. No→Continue.** For example, she tells you to fuck off or calls you a pervert! She is coy and says she's armed—or says she's an IRS field agent.

√ **Does she ask questions? No→ Terminate Yes→Continue.** Such as: How long are you keeping me here? Can I go now? Why are you wearing a ski mask? Is this an alien abduction?

√ **Does she tell you her real name when you introduce yourself? No→Terminate. Yes→ Continue.** Elvira, Cher, Madonna, Xena, Fabio, Yanni, Lassie, etc.

√ **Ask her out. Did she accept? No→ Terminate. Yes→Continue.** Did she hint she is a lesbian, married, engaged, dying or moving?

Review Your Test Results. Are you ever able to reach her at home? Does she return your phone calls? Are you able to agree on a time and place to meet? Does she show up? The best measure of how well the first date went is how easy it is to make a second date. The best indicator of how well the second date went is how easy it is to make a third date. You get the idea. If it seems like a struggle to get together and she only wants to meet briefly in a parking lot and tells you that she's an executive recruiter, it's nature's way of telling you she is not your soul mate.

   Yes → Terminate.

Key Phrases to Monitor. Any of the phrases below are the death knell for potential future acts of copulation:

- "I'm not ready to get involved right now . . . ."
- "Why don't we just see each other for lunch . . . ."
- "Let's just be friends . . . ."
- "You're a really nice guy, but . . . ."
- "I'll call you."
- "I'll go down on you for fifty bucks, G. I."

   Yes → Terminate.

Attitude Adjuster: *The BAD Dudes cautiously recommend that you not accept entourage status in a relationship (basically you get to call but she is never home). In the great web of life you will have been reduced to an E. coli in the small bowel of some woman's life—unless of course you aspire to be a tapeworm someday. Then by all means keep calling her.*

Spawning In The Bio-Diversity Of The Singles Tide Pool

Trying to meet the woman of your dreams in the breeding frenzy that constitutes singles introductions is difficult at best—whether it's through personal classified ads, telephone dating, video dating, computer dating, singles newsletters, singles clubs, singles square dancing, Jewish singles, professional singles, singles to share dinner, Sierra Club Singles, Parents Without Partners, 1-900 Hot-Sex (where in order to talk to a woman you have to keep beating the # sign), or whether you are trying to download a date on the Internet.

First consider the finding of professor David Duvall, who studied rattlesnake mating habits. He notes that when a male rattlesnake heads off to find a female, he does so in a straight line, never veering. *In a world where your resources are distributed in random clusters, and you don't know where they are, it turns out that the straighter the path, the higher the probability of colliding with them.*

For many BAD Dudes, going in a straight line is extremely difficult. It means going directly to where the women are at, even if you don't know. It means going through obstacles rather than around them all the time. What it really means is giving up watching TV all weekend, working 24/7 or getting-off all night on adult Web site thumbnail galleries. And when the snake gets there, he must eliminate competitors, then gently win the affections of the female. It's tough out there, even for snakes.

15

Consider the male salmon swimming arduously upstream. With his dying gasp he squirts a cloud of seminal fluid out onto the bottom of a raging river, over the recently ovulated eggs deposited in the riverbed by a female, hoping beyond hope that his genes will continue. This is the strategy of "quantity over quality." It is competing directly with the woman's strategy of quality over quantity.

Depending on how desperate you are, give it a try. Remember to practice safe spawning. Take this analogy literally. Go down to a crowded nightclub, dog paddle out onto the jammin' dance floor, struggle to keep your head above the crowd, think of masturbating and ejaculating out onto all the inebriated women. Now, before the police come and arrest you, calculate the odds that one heroic alpha sperm will climb up a woman's sweaty pantyhose and squirm its way to an ovulating egg. (Note that men produce 12 million sperm an hour, while women produce only about 400 eggs over a lifetime.) "Yeah, Baby!"

Attitude Adjuster: *"Oh Behave!" The BAD Dudes would like to remind you that the salmon is lucky. It dies after ejaculating. There are approximately 2 million brother Dudes currently incarcerated in the United Sates, many of them getting more sex than they want. Our team of statisticians calculates that on any given day in America, your chances of being incarcerated are better than getting a date and consentually impregnating a woman.*

Facing The Zyloid All Night

In what is perhaps one of the oldest courtship rituals between men and women, the *dinner date*, smart men know how to stare out restaurant windows at passing traffic or study blank walls while talking to women about endless biographical data. This *courtship feeding* ritual in which men offer food to women with the hope of gaining sexual consideration is a ploy utilized by the males of many species to demonstrate their prowess as hunters and providers.

Part of the price for attempting to gain sexual access is picking up the tab and watching busboys stack stenching tubs of dirty dishes, the assistant cook hacking an oyster onto the grill and restaurant patrons exiting the restrooms fondling themselves—all because we allow women to be seated first. Men learn that even the worst table in a restaurant has one seat left that is better than the one in which they will be seated. Of course, their date will be seated in the last best seat in the house.

This parade will continue for your entire dating life, until your death, due to an unsuccessful Heimlich Maneuver, by a sixteen year old assistant night manager, as you choke and expire on the floor of a Denny's eating the *faux* meat portion of the "Free $4.95 Senior's Birthday Special" while your wife looks on helplessly.

Once the relationship is established you must speak up, preferably before you are married. Being in public is part of the pleasure of dining out. Assert your need to see and to be seen. Don't make a life-long study of laminated wood grain veneers (zyloid), decorated by plastic framed posters, as if you were taking an evening course to become a junior management trainee in food service. This is the first step to dating and relationship liberation. Who knows, someday, you might even suggest splitting the check! The relationship equivalent of a DMZ.

Attitude Adjuster: *The next time you go to one of those Chez restaurants—the ones with the pastel tablecloths and strange silk flowers arranged in a deformed vase in the middle of the table, looking as if it's having sex with itself—always let her be seated first.*

Women Are Not Into Action Pursuit Games Or Monster Trucks

For reasons not well understood some women are into WWF Smackdowns and Cage Fighting. The BAD Dudes have tried to outline a few practical hints for meeting women. First off, you can stop looking for a good place to meet women. *There are no good places to go and meet women.* Every meeting is a chance event by its very nature. There is no science or logic that can help you here. However, there are a few obvious do's and don'ts.

Don't bother trying to meet a woman while she is seriously shopping, especially if her mother is buying. You should also avoid the obvious: Gun shops, hardware stores, bait and tackle shops, auto part stores, adult movie houses, live sex shows, tobacco shops, firing ranges, hobby shops, electronic and computer stores.

Portrait Of A Serial Loser. The BAD Dudes have decided to issue an alert. It has come to our attention that some Dudes are scaring women away and making it harder for the rest of us to find them. Warning: Once you turn forty, don't go around carrying a boombox while skating on fluorescent yellow roller-blades and wearing wrap-around sun glasses and hot pink Lycra riding pants—no matter how well you think you stuff them front or back. Don't ever wear a bandanna (unless you are a former farm laborer or inmate) or a jacket with a logo of a professional sports team, advertising that you are a loser who has no identity whatsoever. Don't stroke your crotch or stick your tongue out a lot. Don't wear more than one piece of gold jewelry unless you are wearing Italian loafers without socks and have moussed your hair.

Never drive auctioned police-sheriff-highway patrol vehicles, especially if the spotlight is still attached and the logos have been spray painted over. Avoid driving old hearses, ambulances, panel trucks, postal and army surplus vehicles, HMMWVs (High Mobility Multipurpose Wheeled Vehicle) or better understood as expensive retro-fitted military vehicles for gun shop freaks and survivalists, or any car or truck with 66 inch tires, tinted windows, ammo boxes and a vast array of antennas, while wearing a Marine desert fatigue cap or baseball cap with a golf club or farm tractor manufacturer logo. If your vehicle's sheet metal body pulsates to the deep bass response of multiple subwoofers installed in the trunk, causing other vehicles to veer off the road and old people to give you death stares as if you just put a jack hammer up against the door of a pay toilet they were using—look nonchalant as if they are too stupid to understand that you can't appreciate a fine speaker system under 120 decibels, cookin' to the grunge rock music of the *Butthole Surfers*.

Don't be one of five guys crammed into a car or pickup truck all scrounging for gas and beer money while playing air guitars, everyone off key. Don't suggest to your date that you both stash your grocery carts and "dumpster dive" for dinner, then head over to the Can Bank for beer money. Forget inviting her to "sign" (holding a sign that you will work for food) at your favorite intersection. It's better to go for a stroll along the beach at sunset with his and her metal detectors.

Tattoos on your face, neck or over 10% of your body surface are indiscreet. Ditto with body piercing, scarification and plain old disfigurement as a means of exploring the thresholds of pain and paths of consciousness.

Extra holes in your tongue, nose, ears, cheeks, eyebrow or dick may not be the turn on to women you think they are. Unless, of course, you're looking for a woman who has pierced her nipples, labia, eyebrow, tongue, nose, cheek or ear. A shaved head with rat tail, Jeri Curl, comb over, perm or cheap rug—oh hell, keep wearing the bandanna or fatigue cap. Do not have more chains attached to your belt than you have wallets, keys or knives on your person. Multiple leather fanny packs are not tasteful.

Attitude Adjuster: *Never, never be a clean-cut Generation X-er working as a bank teller, wearing a $200 worsted wool suit, crumpled white shirt, fashionable silk tie you can't afford and white underwear—like some kind of a laid-off investment broker, trying to get retirees to switch their FDIC insured savings accounts to risky high-yield investments.*

Have You Considered Previously Owned Persons?!

A person divorced for the first time is more likely to remarry than a never married person is to marry for the first time. A person who is twice divorced is more likely to remarry than a once divorced person. If you are looking for someone who is capable of an emotional commitment, consider becoming involved with someone who has previously risked one. Divorces, today, are less and less about failure, and more and more about our unrealistic expectations for the relationship to be everything to us, at all times in our lives. Try explaining all of this to a 19 year old woman on your first date. There you are trying to convince her that you are really a previously owned luxury car, and all she can see is a "Rent-A-Wreck" that's six months away from being an abandoned vehicle.

The fact is, serial monogamy has replaced golden anniversaries. Approximately 10 percent of all divorces will be for the third time. This means that we may no longer be able to measure successful relationships on the basis of their longevity. More people are simply living much, much longer. Today, two individuals could marry in their fifties and have a 35 year marriage. Today relationships are more about meeting your needs at different stages of your emotional development than about failure.

Just so there is no misunderstanding our meaning, let's examine a typical adult relationship life-cycle. In your twenties you are looking for a young fox who smokes dope, goes to concerts and fucks constantly. By your thirties you are looking for a breeder with a full-time job who won't embarrass you at corporate functions. After the kids get to high school you want a young fox who smokes dope and fucks regularly, except you can't score one of these, so you find a 40ish type with no children who has an appetite for kinky sex. By your sixties you just about have to settle for whoever will take your money; most of these are professionals. At seventy they are also professionals, but in the health care industry—giving you enemas, sponge bathing you, changing bed pans. At eighty you are lucky if you can find someone who will pull the plug on your life-support, unless they are in your will. We figure that's pretty much it.

Divorces can signify failure, but so can relationships that fail to end. Some relationships successfully renegotiate every 4-7 years, some don't. It may not be any more significant than this. A fifty year anniversary may signal nothing more than a couples' willingness to hate each other or be indifferent to their spouse for an entire lifetime, while a person who has divorced 3-4 times may continue to emotionally evolve and grow in very positive ways. Trying to compare golden anniversaries to serial monogamy is like saying a fifty mile long road is better than ten 5 mile long roads. It just depends on where you are trying to get.

Most of the articles and books you will read about people who divorce have hidden shame-based assumptions. They will lead you to believe that those who divorce have commitment problems or difficulty with intimacy. Then they will tout the wisdom of those who have had enduring (so-called "successful") relationships so that we can all find the right path. The BAD Dudes doubt there has ever been a study that examines what is dysfunctional about long-term relationships. If you look closely, you wil find people who have difficulty with autonomy and independence, who tend to be emotionally over-dependent and needy, and who are fearful of being lonely or without a relationship. For those of you who are disgusted by the pain and chaos created by those who have divorced many times, give us all a break and contemplate the pain and chaos created by all those who have never divorced but should have.

Attitude Adjuster: *Marriages have fulfilled many different needs for many cultures at different times in history. Having a loving and emotionally intimate partner is a relatively new and probably unworkable concept, if stability and longevity are the ultimate goals of marriage. We are simply in a transitional period in which the new ways are being stigmatized by the old ways. This is part of the political correctness of our times. Are you "divorce prone," or "marriage phobic" as opposed to "divorce phobic" or "marriage prone." Who gives a good crap. Life is hard enough. Divorcing never gets easier no matter how many times you do it. We are all struggling, trying to get by and make do. Get married. Get divorced. Have a life. Are you stirring this chaos or is it stirring you?*

Thinning The Herd

Depending on the survey you read the first thing a woman checks out is a BAD Dude's eyes, ass, clothes or asset allocations. However, in spite of what all the popular magazine surveys tell you, women select a male partner, all other factors being equal, based on physical attractiveness. This is true of all species. Males that are bigger, stronger, faster, smarter, have nicer hair, brighter plumage, bigger horns, antlers, claws and paws, who take more risks, have nicer complexions, teeth and muscles, and have more confidence, talent, dominance and drive for success are selected first. Of course, most women would deny that they are this superficial and that inner qualities are more important. The fact is, most Dudes are willing to admit to their superficial attraction to women—really, what other type of attraction is there when you think about it?

Because all things are not equal, other factors may outweigh attraction alone. This is where the trade-offs begin. So your horn isn't that impressive. There is a good chance that if you are extremely successful she will overlook this minor flaw in the biological scheme of things. This is a race that would seem to favor younger men, but a young woman might be more impressed with the financial security an older man can offer than with the buff pecs and biceps of a young stud whose life isn't going anywhere. The charm of a young woman's warmth and personality, not to mention her taut body, might outweigh her dim financial prospects or lack of intellectual promise. These trade-offs are time-honored traditions in most cultures. The really neat thing is that there are infinite possibilities in the selection process, because we are all flawed enough to spend endless years of our lives trying to negotiate for more than we're worth. It's as if life were a convention of used car dealers meeting in Las Vegas trying to hustle one another.

Okay! What does this mean, practically? It means that physical attraction is simply the first important gate in the mate selection process. Doing whatever you can to make a good first impression, with regards to physical attractiveness, will go a long ways toward increasing your chances of having a relationship.

Attitude Adjuster: *Don't be misled by the false and romantic notion that "Beauty is only skin deep." Beauty is as deep as it needs to be—which is good enough for a BAD Dude!*

Stay Close To Your Pack

Given all the possibilities for enhancing one's appearance there has evolved a spiraling escalation of attractiveness called fashion. In much the same way male Rhinoceros beetles and Big Horn sheep evolved enormous and non-functional horns to attract females, you may find yourself wearing denim bell bottoms one year and leisure suits of a color not found in nature the next year. Athleticism is hot now. Tight buns in Gore-Tex and baggy shorts down to your knees are also happenin'. Just keep in mind that your appearance is a key biological marker for mate selection.

You get the picture, the struggle never ends, it just shifts its emphasis and focus so that the unfashionable can be weeded out from the rest. You have seen those National Geographic specials, the ones with a startled herd of thundering wildebeest stampeding across the wild grasses of the Serengeti plain, then quickly a geek straggler is pulled down from behind. You turn away and can hardly watch the carnage: in human terms this wildebeest was probably out of fashion. Anyway, clothing is a system for identifying the socio-economic niche we inhabit, and is, generally, a pretty fair indicator if you are going to die in old age after copulating with many females or be a straggler.

Attitude Adjuster: *The BAD Dudes suggest, for your own protection, that you stay out of The Gap, Old Navy, or any other store that offers one style in five colors for spring or fall.*

Getting Upwind At the Mudhole

Now comes the real startler. In two, three seconds tops, a woman can determine if she is physically attracted to you, your socio-economic status and social aptitude. Now comes the real test. She has to smell you. All the BAD Dudes can say is, lucky for us we don't have scent glands on our anuses or powerful musk in our urine, otherwise we would be rubbing against trees, peeing on hubcaps, and sniffing each other's asses in public in order to attract women. Not a pretty sight. Hey warthogs, you want a female to be taken by you? That means a thick patina of mud encrusting your cracking skin, after carefully rolling in your own urine and feces, then getting upwind on the other side of the mudhole so she can smell you. Not an easy thing to do. This is also where a lot of BAD Dudes get into trouble.

There is a great deal of scientific evidence (none of which is presented here) that *pheromones* (chemical scents) play a significant role in sexual attraction for many species, including Homo sapiens. Typically, the male of the species emits a powerful scent that attracts the female, inviting her to copulate or to go to lunch, depending on where your glands are located.

Keep in mind that women's sense of smell is many times more sensitive than men's, particularly during ovulation. Then they become extremely sensitive to men's sexual musk. Bad Dudes pay attention: stinking like a bull musk ox in the heat of summer isn't a turn on. You are sweating, not secreting. Sweat is from your "eccrine glands," which cover most of the body and make your gym socks and jock strap stiff and stinking after going unwashed for two weeks in your locker.

What does this, practically, mean to you? It means that no matter how much you bellow across the watering hole, stamp the ground, snort, grunt, throw your head side to side or dress—a woman will never be attracted to you if you can't get her close enough to really smell you. This is the process of "deep attraction." It also means that each of us has a distinct "odor print" that is as unique as our finger prints, and that Odor-Eaters and crotch colognes aren't going to attract women. BAD Dudes need to stop overdosing on over-the-counter spermicides (see Canoe, Old Spice, Aquavelva and Stetson here). Do not, repeat, do not hang Pine Tree Scents from the rear-view mirror of your car.

Attitude Adjuster: *It is good to be clear about your species, because in successful relationships couples become more similar to one another over time. You start out innocently, like one of those dog owners who looks like his mutt, and end up enjoying flea baths together. You eventually evolve into one of those couples who wear matching bowling shirts, or worse yet designer warm ups, oblivious to all the people gawking at them. They probably smell good to one another too. Not me, not in a million years, you shudder. The BAD Dudes suggest it is good to remain flexible about just what underwear, hair gel or nipple ring you will share.*

For Semi-Desperate Men Only

The BAD Dudes strongly suggest that a single Dude should only consider mail order bride catalogs and introduction services from exotic foreign lands as an alternative of last resort. However, when the options listed below have been exhausted you should apply for or renew your passport. Warning: Use foreign dating services only after exhausting the following:

geriatric nursing facilities; sex workers; detention facilities for women; residential day treatment programs; shelters for battered women; homeless shelters for hard and skinny emancipated runaway teenage girls (you probably won't be lucky enough to get one of these); grifters, signers, stream-of-consciousness slackers, ravers, gleaners, taggers, boosters, juicers and alienated postmodern neo-primitivist adolescent chicks, particularly ones from middle-class families falling back under hard economic times into pathetic rock, black leather, metal stud bracelets, smoking, spiked pink and green hair, Goth imagery, tattoos, body piercing, high doses of caffeine and conspiracy theories, all the while working part-time and going to community college majoring in Business Administration or Child Development. Check out women who fantasize that if they can't be a fashion designer they would rather be a card dealer or bartender in Atlantic City or Las Vegas for just a few years; self-help groups for church secretaries and organists who run away with the church minister; women Ph.D.

chemists or geologists; retired noncommissioned women army officers; UPS and Fed Ex drivers; women who buy Jeep Wranglers with black and white cowhide seat covers; resentful middle-aged women who gave up their lives to care for their ungrateful elderly parents; lesbian women who have decided they want a family; women who answer classified adds to make big bucks in Japan and Saudi Arabia in "entertainment"; bright, attractive, young women who move to Washington D.C. to work for a charismatic Senator or Congressman, but end up entertaining Japanese and Saudi businessmen; women who write to prison inmates in Attica or San Quentin to meet a nice but misunderstood man; Model Mugging instructors; and bleach blondes who drive Corvettes with gold license plate frames proclaiming "Bitch by Birth."

Attitude Adjuster: *The BAD Dudes want you to know that we didn't have enough time or patience to even attempt a complete list—just start adding your own.*

High Tech Women To Avoid

— Owns a wonderful home and has a large dog.

— Owns a horse and doesn't live on a ranch.

— She's "too busy" and needs "downtime."

— Frequently calls late from the office or in traffic to cancel.

— Drives an expensive sports car or SUV.

— Works 60+ hours per week and brags about it.

— Gets up at 5:30 a.m. to work out.

— Goes to bed at 9:30 p.m. to get up at 5:30 a.m.

— Has an MS, MA, a Ph.D. or carries the Sign of the Antichrist, an MBA.

— Her job title is Director, CEO, VP, President, or Yo Bitch.

— Really believes her job is as important as yours.

— Unhealthy relationship with the outdoors—likes to hike, bike, ski, sail, rock climb, spelunk and scuba dive. She is better than you at all of them.

— Hyper-competitive and hogs the TV remote.

— More computer literate than you are.

— Has her own Web site and is not naked on it.

— Consults Palm Pilot to schedule time with you.

— Is over 35 years old and has never been married.

— She has a bigger hard drive than you do.

— Does not want children and she insists that you get a vasectomy.

— Always prefers to eat out.

— Stops in the middle of sex to answer her cell phone as it might be something important.

If you check three items or more, abandon the mother ship now before the alien creature aboard it sucks out your brain through your dick (if you are lucky). Better yet, call in a BAD Dude crew for immediate extraction and vertebrate reinsertion.

The Advantages Of Being A Rich And Handsome American God

Mail Order Catalog Relationships

Before actually meeting her you get to preview a 1/2" x 1/2" grainy black and white photocopy, on 5 pound, recycled newspaper;

↓

you will immediately select the youngest (18-25) and most attractive women in the catalog; and

↓

correspond, by mail, for months in two foreign languages ensuring you both have a great deal in common;

↓

if you can write, she can fall in love;

↓

you get to pay thousands, possibly tens of thousands of dollars for this opportunity;

↓

not to mention the chance to fly to an impoverished third-world country, or to pay for her visit to the United States;

↓

she will be older (age 35 to 45) and uglier than you pictured: however, you will be more desperate;

↓

she will have endured a life-time of physical, emotional and sexual abuse, and what little English she speaks was probably learned from American or Russian service men;

she prepares meals that will include either rice or corn meal, depending on her hemisphere of origin. They'll include snakes, monkeys, insects, rodents and reptiles with which you will not be familiar;

in exchange, you get to be very smart compared to her, and learn a lot about another culture. You will also develop a useless comprehension of a regional dialect few people in the world speak;

she will not talk back, will wait on you hand and foot, be your enthusiastic sex slave, and generally meet all your narcissistic omnipotent fantasies, *until*;

she is inevitably corrupted by the need to "know" or "find" herself and do something that makes her feel worthwhile. Then you are no longer God;

there is a good chance that she is a psychopath who married you for U.S. citizenship, and that she will leave you and start working at an Asian massage parlor/Latin dance club or become a nurse;

but not until her entire family and five children (she claimed she was a virgin) have legally emigrated. In a unilateral act of foreign policy you have now been providing aid to a small village or town for years;

↓

she has contacted an attorney who specializes in suing rich, smart Americans who take advantage of poor immigrant women.

Attitude Adjuster: *The BAD Dudes say, what the hell, if you have exhausted all of the possibilities in the semi-desperate category, who are we to judge you—go for it! Besides we all end up at the same place anyhow.*

Fifty Ways To Dump A Date

How does a BAD Dude in a state of detumescence politely and discretely extricate himself from a woman's apartment, while suffering post-coital remorse? In other words, you got laid, your dick is limp, and you want nothing more than to roll over and go to sleep in your own bed. Equally as important, you don't want to hurt her feelings. You want to do this without litigation or her getting mad, crying, yelling, or developing a "fatal attraction." You want her to like and respect you in the morning, and be willing to have sex with you, again, at some unspecified time and place. It may also be obvious by now that there is no nice and discrete way to extricate yourself. You are going to have to lie, unless, of course, you're one of those assholes who fakes sincerity.

Post-Coital Remorse Blues

1. As she gets a towel for the wet spot—sneak out.
2. When she goes to brush her teeth because you came in her mouth—sneak out.
3. Say you just found an active herpes lesion.
4. Wait until she falls asleep, and—sneak out.
5. Talk about your aneurysm and how they typically blow out after sex.
6. Fake a grand mal seizure.
7. Tell her that you are having a colostomy next week, and does she think you should have it drain on the left or right side?
8. Hint to her that you are a transsexual, and can she guess which organ you had reconstructed?
9. Say you are a transvestite and you saw a cute peignoir in her closet that you'd like to borrow.

10. Tell her that your wife is pregnant and she gets *really* upset when you are out all night.
11. Explain to her that this sexual experience has left you still preferring men.
12. Talk about your work.
13. Scan the cable TV sports channel.
14. Wear a medical alert bracelet that identifies you as a narcoleptic and says you are not to be disturbed.
15. Ask if you may borrow $200 just for tonight to pay off your bookie.
16. Put $100 on her night stand and tell her that she was worth most of it.
17. Pick your nose and wipe it on her comforter.
18. Share your alien abduction experiences and their surgical interest in your genitals.
19. Say you must call your mother to let her know you are okay and will be home late.
20. Share your fascination with serial killers.
21. Tell her about your collection of snuff films.
22. Describe your add in the back of *Soldier of Fortune Magazine* to provide discrete services.
23. Offer her an investment opportunity in real estate, life insurance or the stock market.
24. Mention her stretch marks, cellulite, varicose veins, or that her butt looks too big.
25. Ask if she has hemorrhoids because your tongue is sore.
26. Say you don't normally get involved with women who have her body type. Not that it is bad but that it just doesn't turn you on.
27. Ask, "Can I shave your pubic hair/eye brows?"
28. Tell her you love her and want to marry her.
29. Say you have to go but promise to call later.
30. Interrogate her about her past sex life and imply that she must be some kind of slut.
31. Ask her out for Saturday night.
32. Thank her profusely for having sex with you.

33. Say you feel compelled to share all of your hundreds of meaningless sexual encounters.
34. Casually drop into your conversation how your last two girlfriends are now missing.
35. Tell her the truth. The device on your leg is really an electronic monitor for probation.
36. Tell her that the loud voices inside your head are saying bad things about her. You probably shouldn't have stopped your medications.
37. Talk about computer programming.
38. Defecate in her bed and explain that sex makes you incontinent.
39. Ask if she would give you a suppository. It's the only way you can go to sleep and that your mother usually does it for you.
40. Ask if she has considered surgery (any type).
41. Start coughing and snorting obnoxiously and call her a "fuckin' bitch" or "whore." Explain that it's your Tourette's Disorder.
42. Ask if she has a hypodermic needle you could borrow, just for tonight.
43. Inquire if she is lesbian. You have an intuition.
44. Explain that you couldn't enjoy sex because her vagina was too loose—so perhaps you could explore the adjacent aperture.
45. Use her toothbrush.
46. Ask what her name is—again (you probably won't have to fake this one).
47. Make sexually suggestive remarks about her Troll Doll or Pooh Bear collection.
48. When she catches you going through her wallet, explain that you were just curious about her mother's maiden name.
49. Mention that you can't tell her your real name because you are in a Federal Witness Protection Program.
50. Explain to her that you left your travel pack of *Depends* (adult diapers) at home and that you feel insecure without them.

Dating And The Law

Tort Law And Your First Date

Okay, let's get down to the *Iron Maiden* legal realities of dating and relationships. First and foremost, when you date you are entering into a legal contract and you need to protect yourself. *Personal Injury Law* has recently expanded to include *Sexual Liability Law*. This means that if you infect a woman with a disease or get her pregnant, knowingly or unknowingly, you are financially liable and can be sued. Prior to a date, you need to get a signed *Personal Liability Release* (see sample included in this book) approved by your attorney. You also need to consult with your insurance agent to make sure you have the maximum coverage on your home and car. Doing this the first time is a lot like buying your first jock strap or rubbers, but you get used to it even if you date less—you are protected. That is the important thing today.

Remember, you can only divide your assets so many times. In numbers theory there is the paradox that you can divide a whole number in half infinitely; in reality you can only split your last dime, and there is a judge who will do it, and a woman who will only be satisfied when that happens.

Criminal Law And Your First Date

Your chances of being charged with a rape have greatly increased. It appears that either men are doing it more, or more women are reporting it, or both. We will take this slowly. You need to know the difference between consensual sex and rape. At one extreme is the currently popular notion that all sex is rape and unconsciously murderous behavior (women). At the other extreme is the notion that all women secretly desire to be raped (men). Trying to narrow this down to enjoyable and consensual sex is very difficult, but as Mr. Rogers used to say, "Let's try."

"No" doesn't really mean no—that's why we have the art of seduction, an exchange that negotiates sexual access to women by men. It is the art of turning "no" to "yes". Lying and deception are standard practice, but force and coercion (physical or mental) are against the law. The mutual ingestion of alcohol or drugs before sex is often a good idea; however, drugging someone in order to have sex with them when they lose consciousness is rape. If a woman isn't conscious and doesn't have an immediate prior written agreement with you to have sex as soon as she is unconscious, it's rape. Trying to impress a woman by spending money on her is okay; believing spending money obligates a woman to have sex with you is a big mistake. Being persuasive enough to talk a woman into coming over to your place (or better yet, her letting you come over to her place) and taking her clothes off is impressive. It's not, however, implied permission to have sex. Foreplay and fondling is not permission to have sexual intercourse. If she changes her mind, this requires you to stop. A woman consenting to have sex with you is not the same as agreeing to have sex with your three friends in the next room. This applies to all her body orifices, regardless of which appendage or objects you use, even if you are married.

A woman who gets drunk with you or does drugs, goes over to your place or invites you to her place, engages in foreplay and has sexual intercourse with you and/or your friends, and then decides afterwards that it was a mistake, was not raped. If she drank too much, used poor judgment or wanted to say no but just didn't, she wasn't raped (assuming none of the facts mentioned above apply). If she had sex with you or your friends because you lied to her about your income, feelings for her, education, involvement with someone else, your age or sexual prowess, or size of your sex organ, this is not rape—she was just foolish. If you take advantage of the fact that she is ugly, lonely, foolish or not recovered from a relationship having ended—this is not rape.

Attitude Adjuster: *This is a rapidly changing area of the law. It would be wise to consult an attorney before dating or trying to engage in consensual sex. This is beyond the general knowledge of the layman. Please Note: The BAD Dudes are currently trying to get our Dating Contract printed on every extra large rubber.*

DATING CONTRACT
~~Rental/Lease Agreement~~

Parties. This contract made and executed this date,_____, by and between _____ (herein called Datee) and _____ (herein called Dator, i.e. BAD Dude).

Premises. The Datee hereby agrees to release from all liability the Dator upon all conditions set forth herein, in consideration of the covenants and agreements hereinafter mentioned. The Datee hereby rents/leases to the Dator the premises known as _____.

Security Deposit. An amount to cover the following costs: first and last date, birthday gift (see precious stone here), holiday gifts, roses for Valentine's Day, engagement ring, wedding band, abortion, and therapy for break-up of relationship.

Early Possession. Ideally.

Conditions of Premises. Datee agrees to reveal her natural hair color, all cosmetic surgeries, her date of birth, abortions, children, her current relationship status, etc.

Maintenance, Repair and Alterations. Datee agrees to keep premises in good repair, including: routine hygiene, grooming, weight control, consult on change in hair color; agrees to routinely shave her legs and under her arms (pubic hair is optional), to dress fashionably and maintain color palette congruency.

Subletting. Hopefully.

Waiver of Subrogation. Dator and Datee each hereby release and relieve the other, and waive their entire right of recovery against the other for loss or damage arising out of or incident to the perils insured on or about the Premises, or whatever . . .

Exemption of Dator from Liability. The Datee and Dator agree to release each other from liability for the following personal liability laws: [ ] *paternity of child,* [ ] *exposure to risk of disease and/or infection,* in return for the following information:

42

Dator's Obligation (BAD Dude)

[ ] Genetic-Medical History Profile;
[ ] Blood Tests;
[ ] Recent Dating History Screening;
[ ] Agrees/Does Not Agree to Provide Birth Control;
[ ] Agrees to provide any past or current civil and/or criminal history or charges pending for sexual misconduct or harassment.

Datee's Obligations (Woman)

[ ] It is hereby understood that the Datee is of legal age of consent, of sound mind and body, in possession of her mental facilities, is competent to stand trial, is able to feed, clothe and shelter herself, and is not currently homicidal or suicidal;
[ ] It is further understood that she is consenting to an as yet undefined relationship with the Dator in which she may consent to sex while under the influence of alcohol, drugs, medications, lies, deceptions, seduction, romance, false hopes and expectations, naiveté, Pollyannishness, delusions, biological clock, hormonal fluctuations, food addictions, sexual cravings, and desperate loneliness;
[ ] The Datee acknowledges that all past molestations, rapes, sexual harassment and/or emotional and physical abuses have been satisfactorily treated;
[ ] It is further acknowledged that the Datee is not currently a member of any women's liberation/consciousness–raising group, has not previously joined a cult, and can't name the lesbian biker bar in the community;
[ ] The Datee does not have a psychiatric diagnosis for a major mental illness, and does not have a *Borderline Personality* or *Multiple Personality Disorder*, has never been picked up hitchhiking, gang-banged, or sold herself for sexual services for less than $150 per hour; all tattoos are tasteful/discrete; and does not currently hate her father or feel intimidated by men;

43

[ ] All monies lent by Datee to the Dator are non-refundable, unless a separate contract is established. This includes: monies loaned for his mother's chemotherapy, his overdue house or car payment, gambling debts that will result in broken arms or legs, alimony or child support, church tithing or a great investment opportunity he couldn't afford to pass up, injury suits for *alienation of affection* and *breach of promise of marriage*;

[ ] Having reviewed the attached State laws, it is understood: (1) that the Dator (man) cannot be sued in court for the seduction of a woman over the age of 18; and (2) that *anti-heart balm statutes* prohibit personal injury suits for *alienation of affection* and *breach of promise of marriage.*

Term. In Consideration Whereof, it is agreed to meet for <u>Lunch at Denny's</u> on ___(day)___ , ___(year)___ at ___(time)___ .

This Agreement is binding from _____ to _____ .

It is further agreed that upon a satisfactory termination of this Agreement that the Datee will sign a separate *Criminal Liability Release* for [ ] Rape, [ ] Physical Assault or [ ] Sexual Harassment for the dating time period.

A separate *"Failure to Show"* contract should be signed prior to the signing of *"Date Liability Release"* in order to protect the Dator/Datee in the event one or both parties fail to show for the first date or subsequent dates.

In Witness Whereof, the parties hereto have executed this agreement.

_____   _____
Datee   **Date**   **Dator**   **Date**

Revelation #1: Debriefing

Okay. It's time for an Attitude Adjustment on Dating. Anyone can have a relationship but you have to be clear about what it is you really want. A former BAD Dude, now on relationship parole (i.e., divorced) called, asking if he could get together with us some evening to talk about how he is not making it on the outside. We responded in a concerned and empathetic manner. Essentially we reviewed the 5D's of life (diseased, disabled, dying, dead and divorced) with him on the phone and sent him a form letter:

Dear Yo-Yo:

Go ahead and confess but don't write and tell us you aren't the perp. The more you run over this road kill, the flatter it gets. Because you have written a great novel in prison doesn't mean you are rehabilitated, it means you are a good writer (ditto with art). You have to show believable remorse, in the face of the overwhelming cynicism and pessimism you will encounter on the outside. Having gotten a law degree or an MBA while doing time is really very sweet, but stay and acquire a useful skill, get punked regularly by a prison gang if you really want something marketable on the outside. In your own words tell us why you should be paroled to come back out and try to become a BAD Dude again.

BAD Dudes

Revelation #2:
Men! and Women?

*It May Look Like A Crisis, But It's Only
The End of An Illusion*

Friday night at Cafe Society, in Dockers and Polos, downing Heineken Lights with double espresso chasers. We try to grease some "art tarts" at a feminist poetry reading at the book store next door. We rap goddess-matriarchal hip-hop, how Ann Sexton's poetry forced us to give up our National Socialist White Party Militia affiliations and to stop reciting limericks. We even put down men. It turns out they despise Charles Bukowski too. One tart goes to get the store manager, while the another gives us the *digitus impudicus* while firmly grasping pepper spray in her right hand. We can take a take hint. We ask her out.

Finally, at the beginning of the twenty-first century, men and women have exhausted themselves in what has been a seventy-year campaign by women to liberate themselves from the bonds of patriarchy. They appear to have won a "Pyrrhic victory" by having created the illusion that they were oppressed by men, and that they have now somehow liberated themselves from the biological and psychological bonds of the feminine.

The silly notion that one gender reigns supreme over the other due primarily to sexual dimorphism (larger and stronger) is simply not true and will ensure us of many more years of struggle and bad television sitcoms. This propaganda serves only to continue to victimize women as well as men. It is easy to point to all the ways in which women have historically been victimized. It's also possible to point to all the ways men are tragically victimized.

Attitude Adjuster: *In the pissing contest of life, the bitter truth is that women have always played an equal role and shared an equal responsibility for the condition of the planet, our national state of affairs and for the relationships between men and women. The real question before us now is—who is going to tell them?*

BAD Dudes Who Suffer WMD-1

BAD Dudes who have White Man's Disease-1 (aka Joe Cocker Syndrome) suffer a common but frequently misdiagnosed neurological disorder, clinically known as *Stereotyped Movement Disorder*. Essentially these are Dudes who can't dance. There is no known cure and it can go undetected until adulthood. Epidemiologists describe it as one of the great unacknowledged epidemics of our time. Studies by the Center for Disease Control report incident rates for the general U.S. population are now higher, for the first time, than the number of white men who can't jump (WMD-2). It is now considered a greater threat to good taste in America than Hollywood or rap music.

WMD-1 has been confirmed by the *Human Genome Mapping Project* to be a genetic defect that is inherited on the male's side of the family. In layman's terms it is best described as an inability to "get down," "be funky" and "shake your booty." This is a disabling motor dysfunction that inhibits your capacity to make your oblate spheroids go in two directions on the downbeat of music like Funk, Hip Hop and R&B. This disorder is clinically characterized as *recurrent, voluntary, repetitive rapid motion, with purposeless arrhythmic motor movement affecting multiple muscle groups.*

It's a painless and progressive illness which can lead to enormous social embarrassment to the family and friends of these individuals and cause innocent bystanders to gawk in disgust and discomfort. Sufferers are often unaware that they have this effect on others. As a result it has been institutionalized by the punk movement into a dance art form called slam dancing (a.k.a. moshing), with various evolving schools of dance such as "drunken spazzing," "circle slamming," "freestyle chaos," and "buggin' out."

WMD-1 is related to Tourette's Disorder which, in addition to the movement disorder, causes individuals to talk uncontrollably (aka Talk Show Host Syndrome). It is not related to people who choose to publicly play the accordion, mouth harp, ocarina or air guitar. These are a separate category of behavioral problems.

Sufferers of WMD-1 have numerous denial strategies and rationalizations for their inability to dance: They will make disingenuous public statements such as, "I don't want to dance, thank you" or "I don't dance"; they may derisively refer to dancing as a regressive and infantile behavior that is engaged in by adolescents and preening hysterics who take up ballroom dancing in mid-to late-life; if forced to they will do the Twist (this is to Baby Boomers what the Hokey Pokey was to their parents); the most seriously disordered are constantly asking friends and strangers to dance, seeking out as much attention on the dance floor as possible—bumping, elbowing and stepping on anyone near them, spastically jerking and having the oblivious time of their lives.

Attitude Adjuster: *Of course dancing is stupid and unnatural, but women really enjoy it. If you want to significantly increase the number of women you meet, learn to dance. The NAACP has a scholarship fund for white males who can't dance, if you are willing to visit inner-city tax free economic zones. Their motto is, "It is a terrible waste not to be able to shake your thang."*

Why Men Believe That Topless Dancers Are Attracted To Them

This is a summary of a two year field study funded by the *National Science Foundation's (NSF)* prestigious *William Proxmire Grant* to study the sexual rites of post-indigenous North American males. After orally ingesting powerful mind altering substances, men believe nude women dancers are attracted to them, no matter how obnoxiously they behave. This study asks one of the fundamental paradigmatic questions of science, formulated in the Null hypothesis—how is this possible, not?

A stratified random sample of twenty-five (n=25) topless dancers (5:30 p.m. to midnight shift and Saturday afternoons) was taken at a topless bar two blocks from the Psychology Department. The dependent variable consisted of the first author (Chairman and Professor Emeritus) and two male graduate assistants (GA-1 and GA-2). The independent variable was comprised of each dancer's measurements. *The Statistical Package for the Social Sciences (SPSS)* "Discriminant Analysis Program" was performed for means, standard deviations, and F ratios (multivariate) at the .01 level of confidence.

In classic field research methodology the researchers (i.e., BAD Dudes) tried to blend in and emulate the population under study as much as possible, in order to reduce data contamination. On hundreds of occasions this meant sneaking into a topless bar (i.e., ceremonial lodge), gazing anxiously about in the dark due to night-blindness and trying to make sure no one recognized them. Without benefit of beer (mind altering substance), they had to decide immediately whether to sit in the back, where it was dark and they couldn't see well, or at the bar in the full glare of pulsating strobe lights. They were careful to make sure no one was returning to the drinks at the empty bar stools, and not to search for change too long, an act which created tension for those sitting nearby. After several years they were able to assemble the elements of this sacred ritual:

• There are three ceremonial nights: Wet T-Shirt Night, Amateur Topless Night, and Lingerie Night.

• The basic ritual consists of young women dancing while men get drunk and watch them.

• Each woman has a dance name and costume denoting an archetypal feminine type (innocent or sophisticated or our favorite, nasty-n-bad).

• Each woman dances to three songs of her choice while taking her clothes off. The men in turn shout, clap, holler, laugh and stare at them, placing money on the bar to denote their approval.

- A DJ plays the music, announces the dancers, and encourages men to "put your hands together for . . . ."

- Each man, in turn, becomes captivated by the dancer as she works her way around to him, smiles and makes eye contact. She gets down on her hands and knees and backs up toward his face, seductively flirting with him. This almost always results in dollars on the bar.

- After each song the dancer stands up, then bends over with her breasts dangling near the guy and picks up the dollars, and if he's lucky, she runs them over her breasts (the significance of this act is not yet fully understood) and smiles at him, then moves on to the next guy.

Preliminary Findings

The most startling discovery was how every Dude at the bar, even those way in the back, believed these dancers were attracted to them individually. For a few minutes, no matter how many times they participated in this ceremony, the researchers believed these women wanted them and only them. Each believed that he was somehow different from all the others, no matter how ugly, stupidly or inappropriately they behaved. The fact that a desirable woman was willing to get buck-naked and up close to them and share her genitals with them in a public place, made each one think they were special.

The researchers concluded that a lot of prostitutes, lesbians, drug addicts, and moonlighting school teachers who hated men were making good money acting out male sexual fantasies, while appealing to men's narcissistic need to be special and unique.

In his last report, the chief researcher had fallen under the spell (to quote GA-1) of "a dancer who won't go to bed with him, but has received most of the research funds to date." She had been designated a research assistant under the contract for tax purposes. Among social-behavioral science researchers this is referred to as the deadly "Blue Angel" effect, in which a powerful but desperate, horny, older professional male tries to nurse a fallen woman back to health and gets taken to the cleaners, personally, economically, and professionally. The psychology department is applying for a federal grant to study this effect.

Attitude Adjuster: *This is a power exchange. The dancers get men to give them money, because they see men as basically foolish, stupid and easily manipulated. Men can get women to take their clothes off for money, proving that they are powerful and desirable, and that is what women really want in men. This is often called a win-win negotiation in business parlance.*

Multiple Relationship Disorder (MRD)

The Diagnostic and Statistical Manual of Mental Disorders (DSM-IV) estimates that this dissociative disorder affects 90% of men worldwide. It is not unique to any one cultural, ethnic or racial group, and appears age related, beginning around late puberty (16-19) and subsiding by early mid-life (80-90). This disorder constitutes a fracturing and compartmentalization of the Social-Self (Ss) in order to protect the Ego-Self (Es) from the emotional trauma of Interpersonal Relationships (IPRs). Research suggests women are primarily to blame, particularly mothers. It can remain latent for many years, then activate in the face of a forming relationship. It is also contagious. Active MRD cases are a "bad influence" on men who are not disordered or are dormant. Women are advised to keep men they are in relationships with away from active cases.

Diagnosis. This disorder is divided into three discrete stages of symptom clusters, that are not considered related or progressive.

Stage-I Disorder. This is the mildest and most common form, accounting for nearly 75 percent of all diagnosed cases. Symptoms include: sexual promiscuity; lying about marital status or intentions to commit; seldom staying overnight after making love; disappearing out of the relationship for long periods of time; being frequently unavailable and secretive; almost never saying I love you; continually checking out other women while on a date;

being interested only in sex; and never wanting to go out. Terms such as two-timer, cad, philanderer, gigolo, and asshole are used to shame these men for their illness. Many workaholics, golfers, fishermen and sports enthusiasts are mistakenly diagnosed Stage-1 Disorders.

Stage-II Disorder. These cases range in severity from moderate to high risk, and constitute about 25 percent of all diagnosed cases. Symptoms include: ongoing multiple relationships; two or more wives (bigamy); high-end serial monogamists (6+ wives); never having been married by age 30; polygamy; and creating power for sex exchanges. Politicians and entertainer-celebrities are high risk Stage-II Disorders.

Stage-III Disorder. These cases are called *Malignant Relationship Disorders* (MRD) and represent less than .01 percent of all diagnosed cases. Typical cases include: stalkers, erotomaniacs, serial killers, pedophiles, domestic violence perpetrators and sexual obsessives. Examples include many undiagnosed cases of MRD such as singer Jerry Lee Lewis, whose wives keep dying of so-called natural causes; Jack and Bobby Kennedy's speculated involvement in the death of Marilyn Monroe; Ted Kennedy's involvement in the drowning death of Mary Jo Kopechne; singer Rick James who was convicted of violent drug-related assaults on two women; author Norman Mailer who stabbed his wife; and punk rocker Sid Vicious who was charged with the murder of his girlfriend just before he died of an overdose.

Treatment. These disorders are not treatable and generally remit over time. Attempts at consciousness-raising, sensitivity/awareness groups and women's self-defense courses have proven ineffective.

Differential Diagnosis. MRD should be distinguished from *Multiple Personality Disorder (MPD)*. This is a related disorder primarily suffered by women that results in many separate and compartmentalized personalities, each operating completely independently and unaware of each other. Most men experience this condition as normal for their girlfriends or wives and learn to live with it.

Attitude Adjuster: *You may be asking yourself, why are they telling us about this? Because the next time you are accused of not being able to commit or are caught fooling around you can blame it on MRD. MRD is a disease. You are not responsible for it or the symptoms you experience. There is no known treatment or cure. You are a sufferer and need understanding and compassion (you will be surprised how many women will buy this). BAD Dudes need to get on the victim bandwagon for their own protection.*

Crossing The "Mendoza Line"

Every generation, BAD Dudes are faced with the same fundamental question: "Have you lived life fully, and what does this mean?" For Dudes of the twenty-first century it comes down to this: *how many women do you have to sleep with to feel you are BAD?* This is a difficult question but we have managed to quantify it in the table below. But first a little background. The answer to "How many women?" probably lies somewhere between zero (0) and as many women as you can go to bed with, which, for contemporary standards, we will call the *Big Dipper Line* (for the 20,000 sexual partners claimed by Wilt Chamberlain, who during his other career in basketball was also called the "Big Dipper").

Of the 853 cultures that represent all of known human society, 84 percent are polygamous. It should be noted in all fairness that most men in these cultures have only one wife. Then one has to deal with the fact that some men (none of them BAD Dudes) claim their wives have been their only sexual partners and that they don't desire anyone else. Others appear insatiable and appear to have no limit up until impotence sets in, usually by their late forties or early fifties. (Please note that we do not release information about our members to the general public. However, legitimate marketing schemes can purchase it through our Web site).

Recent surveys might give us a means for knowing whether you have slept with enough women in order to stop feeling anxious about it. When men are asked how many women they have had sex with, the average is usually around seven or eight. When asked, ideally, how many women they would *like* to sleep with, men stated 17-18, while women stated four to five (which by the way is much closer to the two to three they actually average). Ten percent of American males report having had sexual relations with more than 100+ partners.

Sexual Batting Average

	No. Women	Batting Avg.	
	1	.055	
	2	.111	
	3	.167	
Mendoza	**3.6**	**.200**	**Line**
	4	.222	
	5	.278	
	6	.333–.372	won the
Avg. No.—	7	.389	2000 NL
	8	.444	Batting Title
	9	.500	
	10	.556	
	11	.611	
	12	.667	
	13	.722	
	14	.778	
	15	.833	
	16	.889	
	17	.944	
Ideal No.— 18		1.000	

The Mendoza Line

In professional baseball Mario Mendoza was a marginal utility infielder who spent most of his career on the bench. His batting average of .200 became the minimum any starting player could accept in justifying his playing professional ball. Given our penchant for making sex a game we have combined the two. So, have you lived? Have you had sex with enough women? The answer is 3.6 women. This is the minimum number that says, yes! I am a player, I am hitting above the Mendoza Line. I have lived. I should be in the starting line-up and making big bucks.

Attitude Adjuster: *In biological-evolutionary terms you have a big package (even those of us with small ones who didn't want to take showers in gym class). Homo sapiens have the largest genitalia (in terms of length and thickness) of all 192 species of primates. It is considerably larger than a gorilla's, who is three times the weight of a man. No wonder we are accused of thinking with them.*

For some players a concern has arisen as to how big a bat you need in order to hit in the majors. A recent study concluded that if your bat measures between 2.8 and 7.2 inches, when fully extended (average of 5.1" long and 4.9" in circumference), it's a Louisville Slugger. Hey! Be realistic. If your bat is 2.8 inches and you are batting 200 you are never going to bat cleanup. But you will be able to tell your grandchildren that you played in the "Show."

Male Psychosexual Life-Stages

Age	Erectile Status	Relationship Status
1-12	Pre-erect	You don't know it, but you want to screw your mother and kill your father.
13-24	Constant	Still trying to find a woman like mom to screw. You have killed your father by now, if only symbolically.
25-35	Frequent	Convinced your wife is your mother in disguise.
36-43	Occasional	Trying to find a woman to be the teenage daughter you fear being incestuously involved with. This brings the promise of constant hard ons again.
44-55	Infrequent	The woman in your life looks and acts increasingly like your father, only in drag. Sex is like trying to put a wet noodle in a wool sock.
56-68	Flaccid	You and your old lady have started wearing each other's plastic underpants and Estraderm patches. You now know what the phrase "screwing yourself" really means.
69-74	Forgot	You no longer have real hard ons, you just need to pee with it when it stiffens in the morning. You and your wife get up 3 times a night to pee, snack, chat and check each other's supply of *Depends* (adult diaper).
75+	Epiphanic	Among geriatric ecologists a hard on is called an *old growth stand*. You have now successfully screwed your mother, your wife, your daughter, yourself and have killed off your father, among others. It has been a full and satisfying life.

Note: The average BAD Dude is dead now, seven years after retirement, and having been screwed out of his pension.

Busy Women 1—
Seriously Preoccupied

A BAD Dude is never as busy as a single woman. It's hard for a Dude to understand how busy women are when he has nothing to do almost every night. Most of us are always desperately trying to figure out what to do with ourselves. So we catch the sports at 6:30 p.m., then again at 10:30 p.m. and, if we are lucky, again at 11:20 p.m. We come to hate it that they run the sports at the end of the newscasts. When a Dude finally asks a woman out they may immediately compare calendars. She pulls out a 6" thick, leather bound color coded indexed management system and he has a puny 3" x 5" cardboard bound appointment book he got free from his bank. Unless she is madly wild about him she won't be able to schedule any free time for about three weeks.

When the weekend comes our hypothetical BAD Dude has time to wash his car, adjust the calipers and suspension on his mountain bike, vacuum, sit all afternoon watching a celebrity golf pro am, but never call a friend up and suggest getting together as if he has nothing to do. Meanwhile, every night women are getting together with their girlfriends for dinner after work, visiting family and relatives, or going to a birthday party or baby/bridal shower or attending a wedding. They have gifts to buy, evenings are spent writing letters, cards, thank-you-notes or making phone calls they owe to dozens of friends.

Dudes don't really have friends, not in this sense. A brother Dude is someone who doesn't get mad because you drop everything, including your plans to get together with him, in order to meet a woman you could care less about for coffee. A woman wouldn't do this to her friend. In fact we get really pissed off when women won't go out with us because they are getting together with a friend or have to shop for a gift.

Attitude Adjuster: *Basically it is your job to be available to check out the babes at all times. Now if we can get together with a brother Dude and check out the babes, that's different.*

Busy Women 2— Working Type

No, not that type, the other type. A woman will work longer hours than the most compulsive BAD Dude would ever consider. They will work harder to do the job right, but seldom feel as satisfied or confident that it was well done. They will never miss an opportunity to bring their work home with them, or to spend late evenings and weekends trying to finish something up. They are never late to work and often arrive early, seldom taking breaks and almost never taking long lunches. Most of your time together will be spent listening to her complain about how unfair her boss is, how unappreciated she is in her job, how the politics of the office get her down, how she feels attacked by another workmate, and how her job responsibilities are ill-defined and keep expanding so that she can never get her job done right. This will often end in tears of frustration.

As a BAD Dude you are faced with a universal imperative to offer your two cents and try to help her— don't. Don't encourage her to be more assertive, set limits, make her needs and concerns known to her boss, confront inappropriate behavior and requests, not to work such long hours, to pace herself, to ask for the salary she is worth, to take the vacation time that she has coming, to refuse menial tasks that are not job related, to learn to play the game. If you tell her what to do she will soon become angry with you. Furthermore, you will become frustrated that she ignores your hard-earned wisdom. Women usually burn out and change jobs, only to start the cycle over.

Attitude Adjuster: *You may be tempted to marry her or become involved in order to rescue her from the real world. Oh hell, why not. This is not a bad move in most instances. You are lucky to meet someone like this.*

Busy Women 3—
Cycle Of Collapse

The truth is that almost all women are at some stage of collapse. As a BAD Dude you've probably experienced this in a girlfriend or an ex-wife many times by now. This emotional tsunami begins to build weeks in advance. It starts as an energy and a positive euphoria that wants to reach out, to organize and get things done, to make contact with friends and family, and to complete all the unfinished projects around the house. Then slowly and inevitably, a mild anxiety and hyperactivity begins to creep into her once generous spirit. She has overcommitted herself and is now trying to juggle everything at once.

She begins to experience what you refer to as system overload (she hates that term), and it takes the form of a mild panic and disgust with you. She starts asking in a sarcastic tone, "Why don't you help out more around the house?" or "Why you are so selfish and preoccupied with your interests?" She complains how her friends and family want too much from her all the time, including you. At work she has unexpectedly had to take on an extra project she had not planned on, which you have noticed always happens at these moments.

Right before her emotional collapse she will experience a deep panic. She won't be able to sleep, she will become manic and angry at everyone she promised something to. She is afraid to disappoint anyone, no matter how small the promise, and when she inevitably does, her friends will rage at her inconsiderateness, and it will take months to assuage their damaged and hurt feelings, because they never understand. Even if they say they do, they pay her back later and she knows it. Your relationship feels like it is on the rocks.

You are in a bad position here. She really isn't open to advice, yet at some level she is insistent that she wants your assistance. She is certainly hypercritical about how you seem to have time to do the things you want, while she doesn't. She may even challenge you about being so "damn smug and calm all the time." For weeks you have been trying to tell her in your own way that this was going to happen and that she should slow down and take it easy, let people know that she can't do it all.

Right at the moment of collapse you secretly want the pleasure of saying "I told you so." That you had predicted this all along. You will. No BAD Dude can resist this in the face of being accused of being selfish. For once you wish that it would all collapse on her so that she would learn a lesson and not do this again; you also know that it doesn't always collapse and things work out fine despite her catastrophizing, and that no matter what happens this cycle will repeat itself and that there are no lessons to be learned here for her.

The best you can do is give up a piece of your carefully organized life, where you try to plan things ahead of time, and try to anticipate the limits of your emotional and physical resources. You have successfully compartmentalized your life so that its different elements are kept apart. You constantly work to reduce your commitment so that you can focus intensely on doing a few tasks well. Yes, most of her friends think you are a self-absorbed asshole who is not very spontaneous or friendly.

Attitude Adjuster: *After you have worked so carefully to create this calm and cautious way of doing things, she is going to contaminate it and turn your life upside down along with hers. God, don't you just hate that. This is her gift to you?*

Amazon Women And Female Impersonators

In Greek mythology the Amazons were a nation of women warriors who governed and fought the wars while the men raised the children and took care of the household. They were also known as "men-haters." These ancient symbols were reintroduced back into the popular culture with the Amazonian B movies of the 1950s and 1960s, and more recently with TV shows like Xena: Warrior Princess. Undoubtedly these early films were prescient of the struggle between men and women today, and of men's unconscious desire to be dominated by large women. The BAD Dudes have had Amazon women fantasies for years—it's about time we started talking publicly about them.

Not surprisingly there have emerged tribes of men-hating women among us whose need for a BAD Dude is limited to seduction and/or breeding. We know! Your first question is: how can you meet them? The answer is you can't. They will find you. These women are female impersonators—a hyper-feminine tribe of women who act out male sexual fantasies. They exude the most powerful attractant known to man and are feared by most women.

The First Rank of female impersonators is the direct sex workers: The first tier is comprised of prostitutes, topless dancers, adult magazine models, strippers, call girls, phone sex operators, escorts, lap dancers, outcall massage, sex surrogates, world class courtesans and the porn stars who are always writhing and moaning in sexual ecstasy—fantasizing about being in a reality TV series.

Basically these are the front-line sex workers who are providing men a minimum fantasy at an affordable price. At the second tier are all those women who have at some time traded sex for money. Perhaps they needed a Sugar Daddy or a discrete relationship to help make ends meet. When the *Janus Report on Sexual Behavior* asked female respondents if they ever had sex for money, among those whose incomes where up to $20,000, 5% answered yes; from $20,000 to $50,000, 8% answered yes; and from $50,000 to $100,00, 3% answered yes. They estimated 4.2 million women ages 18-64 have engaged in sex for money.

The Second Rank of female impersonators is primarily celebrities, such as super models, actresses and rock stars who ply the seduction of the sex workers in a more coy and sophisticated entertainment form, in order to get ahead in life (so to speak). Seduction in this instance is what their performances are all about. This includes contemporary dominatrixes (man-hating Amazons) such as Madonna and Cher. There are Elizabeth Taylor and Joan Collins as aging, dowager female impersonators. Then, of course, we now have the young, pubescent stars—such as Britney Spears and Christina Aguilera, the ultimate adult Mickey Mouse Club fantasy. The lower tier in this rank are models in the Sunday newspaper supplements, cheerleaders, beauty contestants, aerobic instructors and personal trainers who all help make our communities such interesting places.

The Third Rank of female impersonators is those women who use their sexual hysteria to successfully marry or seduce wealthy men. They may marry a future President, seduce a Senator, go public with their affair with a Presidential candidate, or carry on with a wealthy businessman. Contemporary examples abound, including:

Monica Lewinsky, et al. (President Clinton), Jackie Onassis (Jack Kennedy/Aristotle Onassis), Princess Di/ Fergie (Prince Charles and Prince Andrew), Rita Jenerette (Congressman Jenerette), Marla Maples (Donald Trump) and Linda Medlar (Secretary of HUD Henry Cisneros). This is not to proclaim the virtue or naiveté of our fellow BAD Dudes, far from it, they have all gotten what they deserved in almost every instance. This is about power meeting power. This goes on daily in offices and businesses, between students and college professors, patients and doctors, groupies and rock stars, secretaries and businessmen.

The Fourth Rank includes those who gain notoriety as femmes fatales, "fatal attractionists," Lolitas and seductive victims. They are hyped in the tabloids, photographed by Playboy or Hustler, do the talk shows, maybe get a commercial or a small part in a Broadway play, e.g., Elizabeth Ray (Wayne Hays), Donna Rice (Gary Hart), Fanne Fox (Wilbur Mills), Jessica Hahn (Jim Baker), Fawn Hall (Oliver North), Paula Jones and Gennifer Flowers (Bill Clinton) and Heidi Fleiss (so-called "Madam to the Stars").

The second tier are small time actresses working bit parts at a McDonalds or Pizza Hut, or perhaps as a clerk where you bank or rent videos. Occasionally one breaks through to the big time—such as Amy Fisher (who shot the wife of Joey Buttafuoco in the head) or Lorena Bobbitt (who cut off her husband's penis). Generally they only threaten to kill themselves, tell your wife or call your boss, leave their panties in your bed, make sure you have a hickey or lipstick on you, call you at home and hang up when your wife or girlfriend answers, harass you with calls at work, won't give you the negatives, claims she is pregnant with your child, never wants to use a condom, lets you spent a fortune on her but never puts out, waits until you breakup a relationship for them and then looks at you as if she had never met you.

The Fifth Rank of female impersonators is that extraordinary variety of girls and women, all around us, those who continually make our days exciting and our lives interesting. Bless them all, for they are the dick-teasers and ball-busters. These women can drive you nuts and stop you dead in your tracks, like some stone cold babe who makes you shake your head in disbelief. You think innocently enough "I would love to fuck her." Many times she is that nice and sexy girl next door with too much makeup, high heels, short skirt, gaudy jewelry and, oh my God! does she have a halter top or doesn't she?, who sits with her knees apart so you can see up her skirt, and lucky for you she doesn't give you the time of day.

For most of us they are those seductive women who seem too good to be true—fashionable, sluttish, sex oozing from them, the way they walk, stand, pout, smile, look at you. Too much make-up, too much jewelry, too much thigh and cleavage, everything is too tight, too short, too fashionable, too perfect and too in control. Of course they're too good to be true: that's the fantasy!

Attitude Adjuster: *You have to learn to enjoy just watching, and if you want to drive them nuts, ignore them. Right, like in a million years. Good luck, you are on your own with this one.*

Really Beautiful Women

Somewhere, someone has grown tired of a woman whose beauty runs only skin deep, or what scientists refer to as a *discontinuous state of superheated, crystallized beauty*. If you are serious about wanting to meet one of them you must be prepared to be patient and lucky. First of all *there are no available beautiful women*. They are all taken, just as you have always suspected. If and when a "window of availability" should open, it is so brief that one couldn't possibly be aware of it. For some women it could be measured in nanoseconds. They will choose you. It's your responsibility to be available, in proximity and putting energy out.

More importantly you should seriously question why this is even important to you. Chances are you will be greatly disappointed with the self-centeredness and "high maintenance" required by these "genetic celebrities." They don't come with service contracts and can be enormously expensive. They have often thrived on or are addicted to attention to their beauty, often to the deficit of developing other qualities. This is a high stakes game you'd better know how to play, or avoid altogether.

The BAD Dudes will go over this one more time for the few remaining pockets of naive Dudes out there who still don't get it:

1. Only two types of guys play this game to start with. Those who can truly afford it and those willing to blow every cent they have pretending they can afford to play. That leaves most of us out of this game.

2. Truly beautiful women don't stay married any longer than highly successful men. More importantly they understand the transciency of their power; it is fading and creating chronic desperation. They require constant proof that they're beautiful, and there's no man alive who can do this for long. If you are insecure, a beautiful woman is truly beyond your emotional comprehension.

3. Their ability to get men to pay attention to them is staggering. There's no place on the face of this earth the two of you can go where some guy isn't hitting on her. Every action of a beautiful woman, even if it involves the elimination of bodily waste products, is seduction to some man out there. You have to learn to cultivate an attitude of indifference or be truly indifferent. But she will know the difference.

4. So you got her a part in a Broadway play, a part-time modeling contract or even a small part in a film, opened the boutique she always wanted, or put out for years to keep her in a nice apartment and luxury automobile. Then there are expensive vacations, being seen at the right parties, endless hours of getting ready, constant anxiety about being dressed fashionably, and questions like, "Does my butt look too big?" That is, unless of course you're able to trivialize her entire existence because you are too important. This is a short-term strategy.

5. She is going to dump you sooner or later. Her new man will be (a) younger and more handsome or (b) richer and more successful—one or the other, depending on which one pushes your buttons the most. This can crush even the best of Dudes. The creeping insecurity of her

fading beauty not only drives her to prove she still has it but to demonstrate that you are unworthy of it.

6. It is always better if you dump her first, and learn to understand that the substantial financial investment you made was a small price for making all those other Dudes envious as hell.

Attitude Adjuster: *This scenario is played out at many different levels. It doesn't matter whether you are a wealthy shipping or oil magnate, prince, sheik, Mafioso don, despot, mogul, famous entertainer or athlete, a guy who blows his entire paycheck to impress a woman or a dumbshit kid who drops a month's allowance at a mall to impress a girl from school. Hey! It's as simple as that.*

Women Are Virtual Reality

The BAD Dudes want to discuss a very explosive subject: How can you tell if a woman is real or if she only a "holodeck" fantasy?! As a Junior Starfleet Commander you are clear about your Prime Directive: Your mission is to score as soon as possible with Star Trek's Seven of Nine (earth name Jeri Ryan). However, a woman's Prime Directive, the Bad Dudes would conjecture, is to look as adolescent for as long as possible. When this is no longer possible she has two choices: 1) a makeover or 2) food.

The Makeover. As an innocent BAD Dude you wander into your local Mega-Mall, put down your Game Boy for a moment, and gaze at all the stores devoted to women's fashion, like a child staring out into space at night. (A Carl Sagan moment.) Why are there twenty women's shoe stores, fifteen jewelry stores, a half-dozen makeover salons and hundreds of clothing stores devoted to women's fashion? Plus there's a See's Candies and Krispy Kreme Doughnuts right next to Jenny Craig. How many times have you got together with brother Dudes and suggested: "Let's head over to See's Candies and score a 5 lb. box of chocolate!"? Meanwhile, you browse Radio Shack, Kay-Bee's, the Nike outlet and leave after 25 minutes and drive over to Home Depot. Now you are probably asking yourself, what are they getting at here?

Why is three quarters of all the retail wealth of our nation devoted to women's appearance?—the BAD Dudes ponder. It's simple. This keeps women looking younger— that's why. The makeover is an attempt by women to say, "Look at me! I am young, attractive, healthy and sexually available." The more desperate would say they have "good taste." But what does this really mean? It means that most women are not what they seem—that there is a distortion in the Matrix, a time-warp in which the illusion of attractiveness is maintained as a sort of holographic record of the past.

A young woman doesn't have to do anything to look attractive; she just is. The reason fashion designers use young, beautiful women to model their clothes is because the young women make their clothes look good, not the other way around. This is a fact that appears completely lost on most women. The unfortunate fact is, for most women, the makeover is nothing more than prepainting the corpse. It's all one step removed from mummification.

It's important, we believe, for Cyberdudes to jack into this multi-dimensional reality of Morphing women before probing their bioports (always use an antivirus program).

After you take away the breast augmentation, nose job, the fat sucking, and the wrinkle removing Botoxin, who is this person? If you hide her lip glosses, lip sticks, mascara, eyeliners, shadows, and toners, would you know her? What if she couldn't pluck her eyebrows, tink her lashes or use electrolysis, exfoliating wax, or hair removal systems, would she have to shave? What does her face really look like when she doesn't use facial rejuvenators, blushers, moisturizers, powders and matte foundations? Does any woman have natural hair? They spend a lot of time at salons that will cut, trim, tint, dye, highlight, bleach, mousse, curl, straighten and style their hair, and all you want her to do is shave her legs, pits and pubes. And why do women paint their fingernails and toenails in bright, alluring colors and patterns, and douse themselves with perfumes and feminine hygiene deodorants? (Don't ever take a deep breath of this stuff when muff-diving unless you have a decompression chamber handy!)

The BAD Dudes want to tell you that the modern woman has mutated into half-Cyborg/half-human in order to keep looking young, to maintain the adolescent fantasy for as long as possible. It's no wonder that BAD Dudes are obsessed with fantasy and that the reality of women can be very disappointing. (By the way, how much would you bid on eBay for one of Seven of Nine's one-piece uniforms after she has worked out in it all day?)

Food. Nearly sixty percent of women in the United States are overweight. If they are not obese, then there is a good chance they are anorexic or bulimic or both. Regardless, most women are left chronically dissatisfied with their weight and end up habitually struggling with food. This process has created a chronic crisis of self-esteem for women, resulting in nearly all women having some form of eating disorder. (You need to seriously think about this before getting involved with a woman. Okay! That's long enough. Let's move it along now.)

This is very tricky for a BAD Dude. Women may start out slender but end up large. If you have just started dating and her ass is bigger than yours and this bothers you, you should terminate dating her. (Think about Seven of Nine's' ass! Careful, if you do this too long it will cause a breach in the warp core!) Also keep in mind that nagging doesn't do any good—no, no, no—so stop it! And neither does having sex with her best girlfriend (we have no formal recommendation to make on this subject, except that she should be the cute one).

There are some practical guidelines we would like to offer. For example, it's important that you help the woman you are dating or married to differentiate between a recent uncomfortable weight gain, and say, for instance, pregnancy, a 350 lb. ovarian cyst or a 200 lb. fecal impaction. Apparently some women are unable to tell the difference. (This should give one reason to pause and ponder for a moment.) A few simple questions will help. Do not try to do more than ask questions. Regarding the latter (fecal impaction), anal intercourse is ill advised. Our editor suggested, "Please, let's not go there." The BAD Dudes couldn't agree more!

In a culture in which women are judged by how they look, it is no wonder they experience a chronic crisis of self-esteem, punctuated by shopping sprees, makeovers, and unending pursuits of fashion, a frantic searching out of wrinkles and gray hairs and participating in the modern American vomitorium called Weight Watchers. (We still have life-size, limited edition posters of Seven of Nine available—arms behind her back, breasts thrust forward, puzzled over what an emotion is.)

Attitude Adjuster: *All of this may tempt you to casually inquire about a woman's attitude toward her body while on a first date. This is a dangerous and inflammatory process that is similar to a woman inquiring about the size of your genitals on the first date. Don't do it. Rather, tell her she looks nice and just keep going to Cost-Cutters to get your hair cut and working out at Gold's Gym three nights a week. Remember, there are thousands of scientists working day and night to create their replicant fantasy (and yours), a Cyborg you can have great sex with. (That's what it's all about—isn't it?!)*

Women's Attraction To Bad Men

The Bad Dudes insist that "victimology" continues to maintain a strong hold on the American psyche and will be a growth industry well into the 2000s. Nowhere is this more vividly portrayed than on television talk shows—the major avenues of forgiveness in our society. Long before therapists had a clue that shame was a significant factor in our collective conscious, talk shows were banking high rating shares by offering up a juicy voyeur's paradisc to audiences titillated by women's outpouring of shame and anger.

At the epicenter of this phenomenon is how BAD Dudes do mean things to women—cheating and beating on them, abandoning them, and basically using women in hundreds of ingenious ways that continue to astound audiences and leave them indignant and angry at men.

Let's quickly review how the BAD Dudes did in the 1990s:

• In modern times, the death of Nicole Brown Simpson and the baseless accusation that O.J. killed her and her friend, Ronald Goldman, overshadowed all other daytime soaps, and has set an enduring standard for daytime TV ratings. (O.J. receives the honorary rank of *Supreme Head Commander* from the Order of Vlad the Impaler.)

• Woody Allen betraying Mia Farrow, by becoming involved with his stepdaughter, Soon-Ye Previn, was better than the film and will endure as an underground classic among NY BAD Dude cinematic illuminati. (Woody received the honorary rank of *Créme de la Créme* from the Order of Stroke Rag Subscribers.)

- The eternal battle of lightness and darkness between Princess Di, having to fight anorexia and for her dignity, and poor Prince Charles, who was accused of that most heinous of crimes, being a bore. (P. Char has been made an honorary member of The Order of Lounge Lizards, Reno Chapter.)

- America's former royal couple, "The Donald" dumping his beautiful and loyal wife, Ivana, for a younger and more attractive Marla, whom he dumped for an even younger women. (The Donald is deserving of the *Knight of the Jaws of Life*, our highest award.)

- BAD Dudes hero Joey Buttafuoco cheating on his wife, Mary Jo, and her taking a shot in the head while he semi-victimizes a sixteen year old Lolita, a.k.a. Amy Fisher. (He has been given the honorary title of *Bushwhacker* by the Order of Loved Ones Doing Time, Attica Chapter.)

- Then there's folk legend John Wayne Bobbitt having his member cut off by his wife while sleeping and later going on to star in porn films. (The BAD Dudes honor him with the *Silver Bad to the Bone fig leaf cluster* and the honorary rank of *Attaché*.)

Except for the bullet in the head and the dick being severed we held our own (no pun intended) during the last decade. But as all the carnage subsides and we enter the next millennium it appears that women are now engaging in a new and more sophisticated battle of psychological syndromes. There is Post-Traumatic Stress Disorder, Battered Women's Syndrome, Repressed Childhood Memories and the counter charge of False Memory Syndrome and Attention Deficit Disorder.

Women are coming forward with memories of satanic cults in their neighborhoods—ritually forced to wash their hands before dinner, having to eat their vegetables before they could leave the table, finishing their homework before watching TV, sitting on the lap of that pervert Claus; the hiding of the symbolic eggs; the eating of "the bird"; the androgynous tooth troll coming into their rooms at night; and their covert and sexist indoctrination by large breasted Barbie and dickless Ken dolls.

Attitude Adjuster: The BAD Dudes say: *"You can't protect people from their own stupidity or stop women from getting involved with the wrong men." On the next pages check out the following soap operas (BAD 1, 2, 3, 4) that you can't rescue women from, but might be able to make a tidy profit out of.*

BAD 1—Some Women Want Men To Suck Their Blood

Some women secretly want men to suck their blood—to come to them in the dark of night when they are lonely and afraid, where no light can shine on them. They've lost faith in themselves. They seek out men who can transform them, who are not what they seem to be, who can take possession of willing unprotesting women, rendering them lifeless. As a BAD Dude you should resist this temptation. In the light of day, these same women will wail to their family, friends and often to the police that they couldn't say "no." They don't know why they did it in retrospect and they are terribly humiliated and embarrassed.

Television shows (such as *Dark Shadows* and the best-selling novels *Vampire Chronicles* by Anne Rice) are clues to women's unconscious attraction to certain types of psychologically powerful men, and the helpless inevitability of these fatal attractions.

The dark side of the desire for merger with men is the desire to be consumed, rendered bloodless and lifeless, to be taken-over so that they have no will of their own—being robbed of life is less painful and frightening than life is. These are emotional suicides. So, "good women" find themselves "swinging" or in the brutal bondage of sado-masochistic relationships, lying, stealing or covering for a felon boyfriend. At the death of their "model" husbands, who may regularly beat them, they discover the men may have had five wives or secret bisexual lives to which the women had no clue. They never noticed that their husbands were molesting their children.

On television or in the news these events are made sickly humorous—all the women victimized by men masquerading as doctors, lawyers, ministers, gurus, and artists. They are able to convince women to do things they could never imagine themselves doing, until asked by the right person! If you are not careful some of these same women can bring forth the vampire in you—make you feel powerful in dark ways you have never imagined.

Attitude Adjuster: *As a BAD Dude be careful! A woman's helplessness is a powerful psychological reality that can transform you into someone who can make money and have fun exploiting women—before they form a posse and come after you.*

BAD 2—This Is So Predictable Criminals Are Writing Treatises

The bilking of lonely-hearts victims (by so-called "Love Bandits" or "Green Card Gigolos") has become such a trite area of practice and so full of amateurs that few self-respecting BAD Dudes bother with this genre of hustle. The classic text on this was written by the infamous Sigmund Engel, who over a fifty-year span married forty women and defrauded hundreds of others, until he was arrested and sent to prison (where he died in his seventies, unrepentant). He laid out the basic strategy for finding and making a mark:

1. Always look for widows; they have fewer complications.
2. Make friends with the entire family.
3. Send a woman frequent bouquets — roses, never orchids.
4. Don't ask for money. Make her suggest lending it to you.
5. Be attentive at all times.
6. Be gentle and ardent.
7. Always be a perfect gentleman.
8. Subordinate sex.

We have taken to quoting him at length here because it becomes obvious that there is a vast difference between a woman being taken by a professional, and one strung out by some amateur who does not know what he is doing. It also becomes clear that there is no conspiracy behind the ending of most relationships. Few men are that attentive, gentle, ardent, cultured, friendly or able to subordinate sex. Which is probably why nice guys are so suspect.

Attitude Adjuster: *Most BAD Dudes are just stumbling along without a clue in the world, wreaking havoc wherever they go, with no plan or agenda whatsoever. They are oblivious to the consequences, which makes their behavior seem so premeditated. The best that most of us can do is to pretend we care more than we do, and after awhile even this is hard to do.*

BAD 3—Go To Prison, Meet A Woman (as in "use a gun, go to jail"!)

If you are extremely desperate, relatively indiscriminate about the women in your life and have antisocial tendencies, then commit a felony and go to a state prison—then place an advertisement in a paper that you are looking for a pen pal or a relationship. For convicts who want to appeal to the incredibly busy modern woman, they can go online at meet-an-inmate.com. At Folsom State Prison in California, an average of twelve men marry each month. Prisoners indicate receiving an average of six to eight letters per week from women responding to their ads. The more heinous criminals and notorious inmates tend to get an even greater number of responses. Keep in mind that married prisoners can have conjugal visits once every three months—which may be more than you are getting now. The advantage for these women is they know where their men are at night and they receive frequent sentient and sticky proclamations from them expressing their gratitude.

This phenomenon applies to state hospitals for the criminally insane and mentally-disordered sex offenders as well. However, in these instances, a female psychiatric technician, nurse or therapist usually is charmed by and falls in love with a patient and marries him after discharge from the hospital. Usually they find innocent psychopaths who need to be rescued. We should all rejoice at this marvelous quality in women, the quality of being able to love any man. Some people (somewhat cynical but keen-eyed realists) may question these women's motives and worry for their physical and emotional safety.

Whether a woman purposely sets out to invite a bad character into her life, or, after the fact decides she has been used, the surest way she can keep the hurt and pain alive and assure that she will never be emotionally available for any future relationship is to identify herself as a victim. In some instances she will be convinced by the victimology industry that this is the only way she can be moved to act on her own behalf, by mobilizing her anger and projecting it onto a man or men. But her healing won't come until she can move past this and see her own foolishness, and get off the backs of BAD Dudes. So what if he was an asshole. The world is full of 'em—get used to it.

Attitude Adjuster: *Three hots and a cot, free medical care, weight lifting, frequent access to a law library, no possibility of a lay off or retirement, good company all day long—go for it. Stop paying your taxes. Make it a moral issue, make it about freedom. Tax evasion is the safest and fastest way to do time. Be indignant, no settlement, no compromises—you did the crime, you want to do the time. You want to take it like a man, not wimp out by paying your debt off at ten cents on the dollar for 20 years. Demand prison time and an opportunity to engage in some real male bonding and to meet a few good women. Vive la révolution!*

BAD 4—The Conspiracy Of Hindsight

The accusation by women that a BAD Dude used her or took advantage of her is <u>always</u> untrue. When you drive a relationship off the lot it's a buyers beware contract—"As Is." *There are no warranties on parts or labor, money back guarantees, prorating based on wear, or "Lemon" laws. This is not Macy's or Nordstroms where you get to return or exchange items without question because you changed your mind. You can't return it in thirty days because you signed a contract under the duress of a pushy door-to-door salesman or high pressured phone sales person or made a great telemarketing deal at two in the morning.*

Nothing can protect you from entering into a relationship that doesn't work out. Feeling used in a relationship is always the result of not going slow enough and of not having established the reality of the other person. Usually we do this out of our own needs, which we are desperately willing to have met at almost any cost.

Many men are not truthful, act deceptively, or misrepresent themselves to women out of their own misperceived self-interest. Some make a very good living at it. Women believe them because they are projecting their own misperceived needs. So what is so shocking or unusual about this?

After a relationship has ended many women will make the accusation that they have been *used*. This is the *conspiracy of hindsight*. As if men have nothing better to do than sit around trying to figure out how to seduce and abandon women (okay, so some do). The truth is, feeling used is the natural problem that arises because anyone can have a relationship.

There is no mandatory testing to weed out the relationship impaired, no sanctioned national examination, state licensing board, certificate of minimal competency, no rating system like we have for movies, where we can be prewarned of sex and violence. It's so bleak there aren't any mail fraud schemes offering the relationship equivalent of a contractor's or real estate license in six weeks or your money back. Just go out and have one right away.

We all enter relationships as if they were a carnival in a mall parking lot, or some grand theme park or Disney World, where you get all the excitement and none of the risk. And everyone thinks they get free admission. The truth is relationships are closer to hiking out into one of our national forests and encountering a grizzly bear while trying to squat and take a dump behind a bush for the first time. Your pants are hanging on your ankles, your thighs are cramping and you don't have any toilet paper. Damn! You hadn't anticipated needing toilet paper. This could spoil the whole weekend. For most people this results in relationships being the primary drama of their lives, only they are out trekking in their own vast interior wilderness, full of its own predators and prey.

Relationships are the great common denominator that makes us all the same—rich or poor, famous or unseen. She comes home and finds he has left and cleaned out her place as well; he denies she ever loaned him money and claims it was an outright gift; she just never hears from him again; he fakes his suicide and later she discovers he has a wife and family in another state; he has fallen in love with someone else, again. No matter how relationships end, quietly or in the tabloids, they all end in the usual ways. Then all decisions made during the course of the relationship, no matter how unreasonably or democratically they were reached, get the scrutiny of hindsight. They come to be perceived as manipulations or coercion, and with having an ulterior and sinister motive. And she agreed because she loved him, or to keep the relationship together for the sake of the children, or because at the time it just didn't seem that important.

The reasons are endless and the results predictable. Wake up! No one just ups and leaves for no reason. They left a long time ago, if they were even there. "Where the hell were you?!" is the only real question here. Probably in denial is where you were at. You are still worrying about toilet paper when there is a bear charging toward you.

One party may well have gotten more of his or her immediate needs met from a relationship, but so what! The beauty of a good conspiracy theory is that it denies the so-called victim's role in this process. Rather than accepting your losses or admitting you've been impulsive or gullible and dealing with it, it's easier to blame the other person. He or she may well have taken you to the cleaners, emotionally and financially. But the bottom line is that everyone is powerless in relationships, and you failed to exploit this reality.

Attitude Adjuster: *Basically, all relationships are tested in the same way biologists test bone strength. "A bone's strength can be measured by determining the force necessary to damage it in a machine." Everyone exercises their self-interest toward everyone else, all the time. Love is often the delusion that this isn't true. BAD Dudes want everyone to get off the pity pot.*

Women's Attraction To Men Gone Bad

√   Some women are attracted to seriously BAD Dudes for vicarious excitement. What they really need are testosterone injections to get them started on shoplifting.

√   A few women feel safer and more protected from a dangerous world by dangerous men. In other words, she can't hurt you but he can kick your ass.

√   They have a fantasy that only they can change him, make him better, and nurture him to health . . . then he dumps her.

√   They feel superior to these men and, therefore, better about themselves, a sort of mind fuck that is often explosive.

√   They hope these men will display gratitude and love them since they are willing to become involved with such bad actors. Or that the men will pimp them, to which they usually agree.

√   They believe these men will be more subservient, easier to control and grateful because they reject societal mores to be with them. No, they'll be out fucking around just the same.

√   Some women are enormously lonely, with little self-esteem, who believe they are not good enough to do better. This is just what bad men are looking for.

√   By embracing dangerous men some women are being rebellious and acting out at parents and a society they do not feel accepted by. Why not just drown your kids instead?

√   They are unconsciously expressing unacceptable elements of themselves that need to be loved and healed. Frequent beatings allow them to join the cult of victims and receive guidance at women's shelters.

√   They continuously reenact "the role of victim" in their lives, unable to face their own issues and find a truly intimate relationship. They just want to leave the fetus in a trash can.

√   Some women are very naive, trusting, stupid and forgiving in ways no man can understand.

Women And The Occult

Has the woman you just met recently vacationed in Sedona, Arizona, in order to take a "Vortex Tour" of power spots that radiate invisible mystical energy that can enhance consciousness, make it easier to recall past lives and communicate with space beings? Have you noticed that women have an esoteric relationship to reality, and that it is very difficult, if not impossible, to have a relationship when the little things keep getting in the way? For instance, *the two of you don't have a shared understanding of the physical laws that govern the universe.* She resides in a world filled with premonitions, intuitions, hidden signs, déjà vu experiences and unbelievable coincidences. Events you view as common-place, everyday occurrences and of reasonable probability, she attributes to a dream, a fleeting thought or wish, or hidden powers.

Women often act as if their psychic life controls the physical world. A friend calls, and they had just been thinking about her, or they had a dream and then they had a similar experience (in exact detail she claims). They will have frequent premonitions that something is going to go wrong or be okay. It is their good thought for their car that keeps it running well, not you busting your ass maintaining it. Women believe that there are subtle psychic principles; that good deeds and thoughts (Karma) result in good luck or wish fulfillment, and that there are no real coincidences, but hidden forces that can be tapped into (Synchronicity). They come to believe that they can protect themselves and their families by seeking out these universal principles of harmony, e.g., by reading the daily astrology column, consulting the *I Ching* or medicine cards, and going along with their intuition no matter how illogical or impulsive it might be.

There is no point in gathering information, becoming informed or researching things. They will maintain fetish objects or amulets around the house, special herbs, crystals, rocks, feathers, incense, curios or refrigerator magnets, and will feng shui the house. And most importantly, they completely ignore all those occasions when none of this works out or makes any sense whatsoever. And they won't stop talking about the one time they were right, convinced some power or force was at work. The BAD Dudes suggest that just because some idiot wins a jackpot at Atlantic City or a state lottery, this doesn't prove the existence of God.

Naturally there is a dark side to all the irrationality and magical thinking that constitutes a woman's emotional wish fulfillment. We get goddess groups that seek to empower the feminine aspects of the goddess within women, women who run with packs of wolves, psychics, trance channelers and mediums who claim to receive messages from alternate levels of consciousness and ascended entities.

Here is the point. Mysticism becomes an all encom-passing defense against intimacy and the possibility of being hurt in a relationship. What the hell do they need with you when they can have perfection? They can now have a personal relationship with an all-powerful entity, spiritual guide or path that loves them and won't criticize or hurt them, and that leaves them feeling more perfect than they have ever felt before. You have probably run into one of these women by now. They are mostly angry, middle-class, white women who have given up the hope of having a relationship with a man, though many of them don't know it yet. They now dream of being medicine women and shamans. The younger ones have not been able to find a wealthy benefactor who will set them up in a fashionable boutique in one of those artsy-fartsy seaside towns, and the middle-aged ones have raised their god-damn kids and that excuse for a husband who died of a heart attack or left for a younger woman. They drum, burn sage in their homes, decorate gourds, buy mudhead Kachina dolls from specialty shops in fashionable shopping areas, and practice the ceremonial rituals of Native Americans. They get to read new-old crap by Carlos Castaneda and shape-change themselves into crows and seek out ally states of "nonordinary reality."

They have undergone a sort of spiritual boutiquing of their consciousness. Perhaps you have had the experience of browsing with one of them at an alternative spiritual bookstore and finding yourself between the astral charts and the angelic technologies, having to hold on to the door jam in order to keep your feet on the ground.

The truth is you cannot spiritually enter into the esoteric knowledge of these indigenous peoples and extract the spirituality from their life experiences, and then package it for the consumption of the spiritually bereft, any more than therapy is going to make a BAD Dude learn to communicate better. However, just to prove you wrong they will get another past-lives hypnotic regression. You wouldn't consider eating the heart of some guy you just blew away, just because he put up a brave struggle. Besides, it is too messy and you never handle the disposal of bodies. Dudes are too practical for this nonsense, unless of course it involves our golf game.

Warning: If the woman you are dating has attended one or more of these workshops in the last six months or if she has an extensive library of related works then, you are about to enter the world of the occult. Take a priest with you, the blood of an ox, a chicken liver—or, better yet, do not enter.

Harmonic Convergence
Astrology in Spell and Ritual
Chara/Mojo/Gris-Gris Bag
Shamanic Healing
Aura Readings
Course in Miracles
Crystals for Healing
Hoova Channeling
Chakra Balancing
Luminescence Seminar
Aura Readings
Lazarus Speaks Seminar
Pagans for Public Relations
Seth Channeling

Attitude Adjuster: *You might want to consider becoming a spiritual guru. It is a great way to get laid and it pays big bucks. It is also spiritually uplifting—it's a good gig if you can get it. Best to consult with Jimmy Swaggart or Deepak Chopra first. Recommendation of the week: Avoid any book written by a former theologian about life or by any physicist about the spiritual world.*

Conspiracy Theory 1A:
Cult Of Women (This is all true!)

ALERT!!! This is a Code Red Emergency. Tune to shortwave radio frequencies for an emergency S.P.E.R.M. (*Society for the Preservation of the Eternal Rights of Men*) broadcast update. We have positive confirmation that there are tens of thousands of biologically armed and desperately ticking gender martyrs (women), who are the first wave for the *Final Solution* to BAD Dudes. Be aware that one in four children in the United States is born to a single woman, and 65% of "single mothers by choice" never tell the father they are trying to become pregnant. Right now they are preparing to *service their targets* and *suppress your assets* in a long-term program for *immediate permanent incapacitation*.

We are not talking about marriage, date rape charges or other chump-change third-world counter-insurgency hostilities. We are talking about nothing less than unauthorized and covert gonadal entry and semen extraction for the purpose of biological experimentation and eventual world domination by *The Sisterhood for Kvetching About Gametes* (SKAGS). We suspect this is part of a vast conspiracy to harvest men as an enriched carbon-based energy source. Check-out our latest Web page update on "The Conspiracy" . . . .

96

Final Solution To BAD Dudes

Stage 1. Sexual Enslavement. Their initial objective is to control us through our sexuality. To repress us sexually so that we will become obsessed with pornography and perversion. In this desperate state they plot to covertly extract our semen under the pretense that we are sexy guys who are scoring big-time on our first date. With the advent of in vitro fertilization it is imperative that all men immediately stop donations to sperm banks.

Stage 2. Financial Collapse. First we will be worked to death. Then they will drain us off financially through palimony, alimony, and child support, reducing our income to below minimum wage, taking our retirement, and, finally, breaking down what is left of our self-esteem. It is a well known fact that there is a plot by the courts, the district attorneys, and the ACLU to track us down and make us "bunk muffins" at San Quentin State Prison.

Stage 3. Emotional Degradation. We will be emotionally extorted for the rest of our lives with the knowledge that we have children somewhere out there in the world whom we can't see or visit. If, by chance, we get limited visitation rights—they will make our lives hell if we try to see our kids. They will sabotage any potential relationship we might form by continually taking us back to court, and accusing us of sexually, physically, and emotionally abusing our kids during visitations. They will seek more money and try to reduce or eliminate all contact by us. They may even marry their lesbian lovers and try to make them our children's surrogate fathers, further emasculating our sons. Our sons will be raised in daycares and taught in schools by them. They will never know their fathers or about being a man. They will have only the hollow presence of the masculine, becoming imitators of the feminine—passive, emotional, and neurotic. This will ultimately result in their becoming violent, and eventually lead to their enslavement (The BAD Dudes say this is not a pretty picture).

Stage 4. Painless Extraction of Our Brain Stems And Spinal Columns in Preparation for Consumption. After we are sexually consumed, financially ruined, and emotionally degraded (assuming we have not been killed by war, become the victim of a homicide, been injured or killed in an industrial accident, or expired from a chronic stress related disease) we will be eaten.

Attitude Adjuster: *Look on the bright side, we advise. "BE HAPPY" and remember that "Girls Just Want to Have Fun." Okay, we were just joking with you. Here is the truth. From the standpoint of human biology and evolutionary theory all men after the age of 30 are reproductively irrelevant. No one gives a shit whether you get eaten or not.*

Revelation #2: Debriefing

As this bitter struggle continues into the 21st century, BAD Dudes have started to evolve a code of conduct to help us cope with relationships. Once you get past dating you need to know your rights in order to help you develop an attitude. This is because a woman will require you to be emotionally interactive. Keep in mind—you cannot develop the right attitude until you have learned to use the word *fuck* in its legal context. Familiarize yourself with the attitude adjuster below.

Review Your "Relationship Miranda Rights"

- *You have the right to remain silent.* Fuckin' "A"! Most relationship problems are caused by talking. You have the right to watch TV, crap in private, read the newspaper at the table and get together and shoot the shit with your friends whenever you like.

- *Anything you say, can and will be used against you*—Unfuckingbelievable! You have suspected this all along.

- *You have the right to talk to a lawyer and have him present with you while you are being questioned.* This makes good fucking sense to you. Being alone together is the second biggest cause of most your problems, next to talking.

- *If you cannot afford to hire a lawyer one will be appointed before any questioning.* You wonder if he/she will be interested in a three-way after you reconcile. You know an attorney is going to fuck you somehow, why not try to enjoy it.

- *I understand my rights and I voluntarily and knowingly give up my rights.* You need an attitude fucking first. Don't give up nothing. Let the police come out and cuff you at home or at work and make it look like you were forced to talk.

Attitude Adjuster: *Yes, you are truly fucked now, and you have our heartfelt sympathy and admiration. However, if you can no longer afford your dues we will be forced to terminate your membership. But who said developing the right attitude would be easy. Be aware that it all gets harder from here on in. Read on.*

Revelation #3:
Sex or Love?

*This Is A Zero-Sum Game You Can't
Refuse To Play*

Saturday night we wander, sobriety deprived, into a dykes on bikes bar trying to pick up motorcycle sluts with outrageous tattoos. One of us take a shot from a butch lesbian in leather chaps and chrome metal studs to the perineal nerves, innervating the groin and the pudenda. As he crawls across the bar floor an excruciating pain radiates throughout the scrotal sac all the way up into his abdomen—we now know God is not a man and hope he isn't a woman. The brother Dudes run for the door, we hear shouts—"let's get medieval on these punk ass bitches—get the Grand Inquisitor." We run, limp for the door being chased by the largest detached rubber appendage we had ever seen. Outside they are busting up our bikes. The rape crisis center reassures us that it will not be necessary to check for sperm. Later that night at a video arcade we console one another that there is a metaphor in all of this.

The third revelation is that all M-F relationships have their analog in the underlying laws governing the universe. Relationships are seen as a microcosm of this whole, and within chaos are elements of order, which you may experience as a woman agreeing to a date and actually showing up; leading to a second date, then to a third and so on; you move in together, become engaged, get married, raise a family and then you divorce, leaving you questioning if there was ever any order in the universe.

The Buddhists saw this as the clash between two great irrepressible forces in the universe, between chaos and order, between Yin and Yang or the feminine and masculine. One can never overcome the other. If there is an imbalance of one over the other it will right itself no matter what the cost, even if it fractures the entire world into unstable subatomic particles. This may have been what the "Big Bang" was all about fifteen billion years ago. One force can never dominate or win out over the other in the long run.

Attitude Adjuster: *This is a zero-sum game. Your homeboys are telling you to check it out. You have to play. It is what defines you, what brought you into the world and formed you. However, if you aren't a Buddhist then this is all just meaningless crap.*

Notes From The Sexual Underground

How can it be, the BAD Dudes opined during a late night, mid-week mind grope—that while women claim to be sexually oppressed by men, what men think of as sex doesn't count for diddly? The feminine standard of sexuality (erotica) is the politically correct one, while the masculine definition (hard core action) meets if not exceeds most community standards for obscenity. The BAD Dudes would like to discuss sex without guilt. For those of you who are offended by the big nasty, don't look now but we are going to take it out and play with it.

NOTE I. Do You Like Exotic Naked Women Performing Unnatural Acts In Public Performances? If you answered yes to this question, then you can rest assured that you are a perfectly normal BAD Dude, no matter how much effort is devoted in your lifetime. (And there will be a great deal of effort to convince you that this is not politically correct). You do not have to harbor deep dark secrets or perversions because you are a sexual person who sees sex everywhere and in everything. In most men testosterone secretions peak six to seven times each day. There is nothing wrong with relating to others through a stream of consciousness that consists primarily of sexual innuendos. You are not a pervert. Everything is a sexual object to a man, including sex. To paraphrase Freud, if it is longer than it is wide it is a phallic symbol, and, we might add, so is everything else.

There is nothing wrong with you because you laugh when a woman says "that is right up my alley." Perhaps you wonder about the phrase "tit for tat," and you like the idea of "naked power." You want to be the "member at large" for your townhouse association or anyplace else for that matter. At work you are bemused when a woman asks you "when do you get off," or "are you coming," not to mention how often you are "tied up at work" or are described as "hard at work." What about coming in on Monday morning and talking about the "tongue and groove" work you did over the weekend. Or the store clerk who shouts at you waiting in line—"I'll take you right here." This has all gotten so ridiculous and out of hand. Think about how self-conscious you would feel sitting around with a group of women complaining about the federal recall of their "electric worm probers" due to electrocutions.

There is a significant portion of our society committed to the proposition that sex is not good for you or for women. It is safe to assume that these people are either repressed, asexual, non-orgasmic or really like it furtive and dirty. From the religious right there is the unending drum beat that sex is a sin, except between consenting married adults, in the missionary position for the purpose of begetting. Unless of course they are priests or ministers, then they can have all the sex they want with prostitutes, children, and the wives they counsel in their congregations or parishes.

With feminism has come a new twist to sexual puritanicalness. Women are being told to take charge of their bodies and sexuality, but also that sexuality, whether for recreation or procreation, is a male conspiracy to dominate and control them. Here is the twist: the new message to women is that lesbianism is the only safe expression of female sexuality. Women are free to have multiple orgasms but preferably with a vibrator or another woman. In this scenario, men are the secular equivalent of the Antichrist.

But not to worry, sex isn't going away any time soon, because the more we try to repress and control sexuality the dirtier and more interesting it becomes. Hallelujah, brothers and sisters, it looks like we are going to keep sex interesting for a long time to come—cheerleaders, pom-pom girls, women at the beach or poolside in string bikinis and skintight one piece suits that are see through when wet, beauty pageants, fashion shows, lingerie ads in the Sunday supplements, plunging necklines, miniskirts, halter tops, braless fashions, erect nipples and silk blouses, women working out in leotards and tight pants, jogging, bicycling, playing volleyball, roller skating, doing yoga on late night TV, bending over, crossing and uncrossing their legs, sliding out from restaurant booths, trying to get out of a sports car in a tight skirt—Women.

NOTE II. Cheap, Sleazy Sex Is Its Own Reward. We often stay in bad relationships for the great sex. But where do you draw the line? She may have the world's largest, most easily identifiable and prolific G-Spot. Does she teach Kegel aerobics? Does her book collection include *S&M—The Last Taboo, Machosluts* or *Physical Interrogation Techniques*? Does she have a dildo with a collection of attachments that would make a Kirby vacuum cleaner salesman blanche? Is her conversation in bed sprinkled with terms you have never heard of before, such as "CBT" (cock and ball torture), "D&S" (dominance and submission), and "erotic power play?" Does she want to play "water sports" (urine and enemas)? Does she have a dresser drawer with a ball gag, butt plunger, cock rings, dildo harness and a spreader bar? What is a man to do about women's emerging sexuality?! However, if she ever mentions "cutting" or "electricity" and plugging you into the wall as a way to experience God, make an excuse to end the date early. Immediately contact Amnesty International, who monitors former third world death squad members who may have escaped to the United States. Watch *America's Most Wanted* for possible rewards.

NOTE III. Really, How Often Do Women Suggest Anal Intercourse Or Want To Shave All Their Pubic Hair? They almost never suggest that their best girlfriend get in bed with the two of you. They seldom enjoy your fantasizing during sex that she is her sister, and are usually disgusted by your desire to interject sexual fantasies into your love life. It leaves them wondering why having sex with them is not enough for you. How often do they come home after work with groceries and an adult video featuring two hours of nonstop gang-banging? They never stand around magazine racks or sex arcades looking at nude pictures of men, or poke holes in bathroom walls, or install two-way mirrors in restrooms.

Obviously there is a significant difference in how men and women express their sexuality. Men like to go to bottomless and topless bars, outcall massage parlors, and escort services, and frequent prostitutes and call girls, or at least fantasize about it. Women on the other hand like to be paid to pose and dance naked, talk dirty and provide sex for the right price. There is even some suggestion that men are the perverts here, and we say, wait just one dang minute there—there is nothing wrong with wearing women's panties—they feel good, especially when you have to sit for hours and play with your laptop porno software program, connect your modem to 1-900 Hot-Sex Talk, or rub against an inflated sex doll. Let's admit it, it is hard to explain to women your sexual fascination with women amputees, beyond its obvious unconscious symbolic representations of male castration anxieties and a need to overcome your counterphobic reaction. But beyond its therapeutic benefits it might feel interesting too. So *what* if men are more polymorphous. Enjoy it, Dude!

NOTE IV. Looking Up A Woman's Skirt Or Down Her Blouse Is A Two-Way Street. Studies in human sexuality and evolutionary biology all suggest that men are more sexually stimulated visually than are women. As a result, men are more interested in naked women than women are in naked men. Men purchase nearly all the XXX rated videos. Most nude magazines cater to male tastes, as do nearly all live sex shows, not to mention men are first to suggest making naked home videos or buying binoculars to watch the neighbors. Visual acuity in men is important in mate attraction and selection, which explains why women are objects of beauty in our culture, with an overemphasis on fashion and appearance.

Men are more voyeuristic, women are more exhibitionist. This is graphically demonstrated by the fact that not many women get arrested for peeping. However, very few men with 55FFF breasts, in a see through halter top, run onto a major league baseball field during a national telecast to kiss the left fielder. This also explains why men go on a date and then reflexively check out every woman who walks by, as if they are unable to control themselves. Most men can't, or are only able to with a great deal of effort. Women shouldn't take this personally. It is almost always the guy who wants to leave the lights on when he is making love, and the woman who wants them off. He wants to see, while she wants to imagine and sense her sexuality.

All magazines sell better when there is an attractive woman on the cover. Female sexuality sells everything better and brings immediate attention to whatever is being sold. So, don't stop watching women's figure skating or beauty pageants, don't be shamed into feeling bad about your voyeuristic interests—it is natural. If you want to stop staring, do it because you are being manipulated by the entertainment industry—check out some of your local talent, who are always bending over or uncrossing their legs as they get up. Why else do women wear short dresses, tight skirts, loose blouses, stretch nylon cycling pants, thong bikinis and—however, be careful not to leer up or down a wrong-way street.

Redbook "What Is Penis Envy?" Quiz

1. Six hundred million TV viewers worldwide watching Michael Jackson grab his crotch 53 times during Super Bowl XXVII (1993).

2. Three hundred old men in gray suits at a psychoanalytic convention in Bern, Switzerland, in late August, trying to figure out, theoretically, why they aren't getting any.

3. A conspiratorial feminist theory that blames Sigmund Freud for discovering that women don't have penises.

4. How you feel about someone making $200/hour.

5. A best-selling line of dildos and sex aids, marketed by "Penis Envy," a transvestite protégé of the late Divine.

6. A pissing contest between psychoanalyst Jeffery Moussareff Masson and *New Yorker* writer Janet Malcolm.

7. What gawkers feel when they see you in your "Big Johnson" T-shirt.

8. What many women felt when Lorena Bobbitt cut off John Wayne Bobbitt's dick with a kitchen knife.

9. A man angrily grabbing his crotch signifying to someone he is having a spat with that, yes, I too have larger than ordinary genitalia and am a BAD Dude.

10. You don't know what penis envy is, don't give a shit, don't know anyone who does, and are tired of hearing about it.

The correct answer is No. 10.

NOTE V. Let's Face It, Men Are More Perverted Than Women. More Dudes: 1) crossdress (transvestites), some rather untastefully we might add; 2) hope to star as female impersonators (a good prison job if you are doing more than ten years, have a youthful look and a tight, boyish ass); 3) surgically alter their sexual gender (transsexuals), you've seen those big-boned, deep-voiced types who look womanlike; 4) are homosexual (i.e., have signs in their bedrooms that state: "Enter in the Rear"); 5) exhibit their genitals without being asked or paid to; 6) engage in voyeuristic acts (which is every man who looks at a woman, *believe us*); 7) commit acts of molestation, incest and rape; 8) engage in sexual fetishes; 9) watch pornography; 10) try to convince their wife or girlfriend to swing; 11) initiate sadistic-masochistic sex acts in relation-ships; 12) want to be little boys who get spanked for being naughty; 13) are turned on by snuff and torture films; 14) have sex with animals (zoophilia); 15) lose objects up their rectums and must go to emergency rooms; 16) make obscene phone calls; 17) publicly touch the opposite sex for sexual arousal (frottage); 18) cheat on their spouses; 19) commit polygamy; 20) go to topless bars, frequent prostitutes, experience an obsessive and unrequited fascination for a woman; 21) stalk women; 22) kill themselves or women trying to experience sexual highs; 23) commit serial and mass murders that have sexual motives; and 24) become members of team sports so they can pat each other's asses.

Now you may ask, so what? What is the big deal here? Boys will be boys. But, something is going on, and many theories have been put forward—it's the deadly Y chromosome (XY) or an extra Y chromosome (XYY), or that men are simply genetically inferior women. The BAD Dudes believe it has a lot to do with rogue testosterone, a chemical hormone primarily about aggression and dominance, which adult men have in amounts ten times greater than women (men have 300 to 1,000 nanograms of testosterone per deciliter of blood, while women typically have 40 nanograms). Let's give biology its due. May the Force be with you, without being turned to the Dark Side. Safe journey, young Jedi Dude.

Basically, today men are getting screwed without sex. Which, by feminist ideals, ought to make us candidates for sainthood. So what really lies behind the pathologizing of men and the feminization of sex in our culture? Don't get paranoid, but it's just what you have suspected all along— a conspiracy to insure that men don't have a good time. Unfortunately for women, being the victim is not nearly so interesting, exciting or financially rewarding as being a man.

Attitude Adjuster: *If your idea of sex is trying to help a woman achieve an orgasm with a vibrator—the twelve volt, 200 amp, AC/DC, 1,500 rpm, self-cooling and lubricating diesel model, with winch, integrated circuitry and microprocessor, electronic ignition (optional kick-start), exhaust fan and drain pan for emissions control, which you are always burning out—this is no longer sex. You are drilling for oil in the North Sea without workman's compensation or a death benefit. If you are getting tired of always watching the horizon from the top of the derrick for a tsunami, it may mean giving up your preoccupation with drilling as your primary contribution to the relationship.*

The Myth Of The Big Green One
Cucumis Sativus
Family: Cucurbitaceae
Genus: Cucumariidae

- *L. Cucumis cumbers* are fruits and they are green!

- Interspecies sex is an ugly thing ($ for photos).

- It's embarrassing to watch women in the produce section fondle dozens of cucumbers, trying to find a hypertrophied cuke, then stand in the Express Line at 10:30 p.m. on a Saturday night with one cucumber and a quart bottle of Mazola Oil.

- They can become habitual and make a woman's vagina wobbly after prolonged and extended use.

- They don't vibrate and you can't add attachments.

- Do you really know who has handled them? And what exactly are those gnarly growths?

- You have to wait until they reach room temperature.

- Is bigger really better? (All right, forget this one)

- Who can you tell that you got cuked last night?

- The current market price of cucumbers exploits farm laborers and is hurting American farmers. Think before you lube your next cuke.

- Is your green one organic?

- Shouldn't you put this sexist urban myth behind you, where it belongs?

- *Remember Purgamentum Init, Exit Purgamentum* (Garbage In, Garbage Out).

Dudes Getting Their Act Together On Love

It's late and we all have to go to work in the morning, but damn it, someone has to say it—there has evolved a post-modern historical deconstructionist revanchism of interpersonal relationships—in other words, "love" has been reduced to a meaningless reciprocation of feelings and thoughts, without enough lubrication (if you get our drift).

To make our point, take this simple test: What is love? (a) buying flowers and saying I love you whenever it counts or (b) working your ass off being a devoted spouse and provider. Hint: Men who answer "b" are like plankton in the feminine food chain, swallowed up, digested and excreted back into the ocean (sometimes the digestive stage is skipped). In order to help make you a shark in this feeding frenzy you need tough love. Read on.

LOVE 1. There Is No Love, Get Over It! Let's get all the nonsense about love out of the way once and for all. Basically, there is no such thing as love between adults. Between adults there is co-dependency, promiscuity, serial relationships, affairs, boredom, great sex, no sex, enmeshment, marriage, dysfunction, romantic intoxication, affection, commitment, and deep caring—nope, can't find any love. Once you have been around long enough you begin to realize that you don't know anyone in love, never really knew anyone in love, never saw anyone in love, never knew anyone who knew someone or had heard of someone in love, and that you yourself have never been in love, and now don't want anything to do with it. It is probably fairly safe to say that most of us wouldn't recognize it if it existed. And it is really frustrating because you keep trying to figure out how to have it. Books, magazines, movies, television, and the recording industry keep trying to sell it to you, and would just about dry up and blow away if the word love disappeared.

You may be asking yourself, if it's not love what is it? Good question. The idea of love has been so degraded as a concept as to be rendered meaningless. We love everything and have bumper stickers to proclaim—"I LOVE MY . . ." (dog, cat, car, country, school, company, musical instrument, ass). Love has become a universal expression for a multitude of feelings and emotional states we are somehow failing to articulate. While the Kayap tribe in the Brazilian Amazon region have about 100 different words for diarrhea, we have one word for the hundreds of emotional states and conditions termed love. Now which is the more sophisticated and civilized culture?

By contemporary standards anyone can love anyone else or anything. We are here to tell you this is crazy and you shouldn't believe it. People talk about how they really "love" this chicken fried steak, or they "love" how this golf club feels in their hand, or they say "love you all," or "isn't that lovely." There is that wonderful all-purpose euphemism "making love," and the favorite expression of men "I love you too," the patronizing "love too sometimes dear," and that favorite expression of women, "I love you, but I am not in love with you,"—say what?! Rather than calling everything love, maybe it is time we stopped calling anything love. It has been rendered meaningless. It falls in the same category of mass hysteria as syringes in soft drinks, satanic cults and alien abductions.

LOVE 2. Love Is Obsession (No, not the perfume).
First off, the woman you have been looking for doesn't
exist. Who is your second choice? That mythical creature
dwells only in your fantasies, on MTV rock videos, and in
the *Sports Illustrated* Swimwear edition, etc.—you get the
picture. Your fantasies are *not* real people, which means
there is a delusion throughout the land as we continually
act as if fantasy or illusions are reality—this is why so
many men engage in unrequited love. You know, it's where
you fantasize that if she really knew you she would love
you. It typically has no intimacy or only imagined intimacy
and there is no relationship to speak of (this probably
sounds good to you if you could just have sex).

Unrequited love is the pursuit of someone who is
distant, a romantic notion perpetuated in film and in
books in our culture, but it has little or no basis in reality
(What's the point? you are asking). It is similar to
gambling in a state lottery where you have a one-in-250
million chance once a week. You could win, but it has an
extremely low probability. This *all or nothing strategy* is
typical of losers. Granted, everyone can't have good self-
esteem, so what are they supposed to do? We suggest they
just pack it in, work longer hours and let the rest of us
procreate for them.

For those of you who see a conspiracy in all of this, try
chanting the mantra below. We teach this in our BAD
Dude Seminars for men who continually fall in love with
unavailable women and aren't willing to give it up for the
rest of us.

For Those Still Not Clear On The Concept

- Sex is not love
- Jealousy is not love
- Unrequited longing is not love
- Hitting someone is not love
- Double suicide pacts are not love
- Stalking a person is not love
- Murdering your spouse or girlfriend because she is leaving you is not love
- Hell! Love is not love.

LOVE 3. Love Is Time+Space. For men the best analogs for understanding emotional distance are *time* and *space*. It is as basic as this—the more miles apart you are and the less time you spend together, the less emotionally available you are for one another—no exceptions, not even for work or careers.

So you have a friend who is always complaining that the women he meets live in a different area code or zip code. Or they are always dating someone who conducts three-month expeditions into the Amazon rain forest five times a year. And, always, just as one becomes serious the other becomes uninterested. This is the dance. The sense of longing these relationships create—the passionate e-mail exchanges and great phone sex. Their unavailability also creates a safe distance that assures that both of them can pretend they have a relationship.

The signs are always there right from the start. Your willingness to ignore them simply means *you* need the distance as well. These *virtual* relationships inoculate those in them from loneliness when they are unable to directly mediate intimacy in their lives. This isn't good or bad, but it is important not to get strung out on a relationship like this when you actually require more intimacy. Getting seriously involved with someone who needs 1,200 miles while you require constant handholding, or who can only tolerate a maximum of six hours of contact per week while you need 50 hours, is probably not a good idea—no matter how great the sex. Be aware of whether your emotional programming operates under significantly different specifications.

In the past you had to hollow out the relationship in order to create a safe space. Now we can literally enact our needs in real time and space. The spectrum of detached and emotionally distant relationships that qualify as relationships today speaks to the ingenuity and adaptiveness of twenty-first-century men and women.

LOVE 4. Love Is Getting Greased At A Car Dealership. Okay, let's really get down to it. Let's toss the lace panties and Jockey briefs on the silk sheets. The legacy we have regarding relationships and romantic love is expressed exclusively in transcendental terms. The idea of love is so elevated that it seldom speaks to the many practical realities and decisions we confront daily. Economic theory more than any other field of study is ideally suited to identifying the role of "self-interest" in the relationship marketplace. It is so wonderfully hard and cold in its findings and conclusions.

First of all, we need to understand that we are all competing in a relationship marketplace dependent on supply and demand. Each of us is both a commodity and a consumer in this marketplace. Relationships are first and foremost economic equations about power and money and the negotiation of one's value in the marketplace. In its grossest terms the relationship negotiation between men and women can be seen simply as bartering *success* for *beauty* or even more reductionistically *money* for *sex*. What you should note in this equation is that women tend to have more intrinsic value than men. Biologists are clear about this. A man is biologically irrelevant by age 30. You are used up from an evolutionary standpoint and must be able to demonstrate your value.

Attitude Adjuster: *For a man, failure in the world of work is tantamount to failure with women, limiting his access to them. The best way for a man to succeed in meeting women is to be successful at what he does.*

But it is much more complex than this, as noted by Hapgood in his book *Why Males Exist:*

> *If females and males were partners in a construction project, females would be imagined as putting up the capital, hiring the subcontractors, acquiring the necessary materials, arranging for permits, and devising half the design changes. The male contributes half the design changes and collects 50 percent of the profit.*

What Hapggood has discovered in evolutionary-biologi- cal terms is that men typically represent the *supply side of the curve*, bringing to the bargaining table power, status, protection, income and their genes, while women typically represent the *demand side of the curve*, bringing physical beauty, sexual access, the continuation of the male genes through children, and emotional support. This isn't to argue that they are equal or that this is fair. It's simply a matter of someone having something you need or want that determines its value.

So what are women demanding in the marketplace, you ask? The newspapers and TV talk shows are full of women complaining that men are not emotionally available to them. "What is wrong with men?" they ask. The answer is: nothing. If women really wanted emotionally available men, men would do it in a second. This is about supply and demand. At present men are simply providing women with what they are selecting for— men who are unavailable because of long work hours, dedication to a career, achievement, ambition and success—because it provides the security and status women seek. These men are in large supply. Men who are distant because that is all women really know about men and because their fathers were never available to them, are also readily available. The fact is, women are always going into a store and buying shoes that don't fit and they wear them—the BAD Dudes suggest they learn to do the same with men.

What can you afford? is the important question. There are fewer attractive women (see XFL Cheerleader types) than men competing for them. This forces up their value. You probably can't afford one of them anyhow. They are not interested in you any more than you can afford to buy a small island. However, there are a lot of high quality women out there. In fact there is an oversupply on the market place, which tends to force their value down. The problem from the psychological standpoint is that too many BAD Dudes, as a result of a glut of good women on the market, overprice their product and can't find a market for it. You need to take your relationship inventory, determine the value of your capital assets, carefully study the market and then make the best investment you can afford and hope that it appreciates.

For advanced BAD Dudes, who have a real relationship, you have driven the car off the lot "As Is." You will eventually become dissatisfied with the woman you are involved with, constantly finding something wrong with her, always feeling that you could find someone better, more attractive, competent, sexy, less complex and emotional, more accommodating and understanding—you could save thousands of dollars and hundreds of hours of couples therapy by acknowledging you got what you could afford. If you appreciate in value over time and she depreciates or her value doesn't rise at the same rate, you will then have to choose whether or not to trade up. This is euphemistically called outgrowing your partner or growing apart—keep reading.

LOVE 5. Love Is For Losers. Romantic love is neurotic at best and psychotic at worst. It's time for BAD Dudes to grow up. We are going to rip you a new heart here, but it's for your own good. If a woman is troubled enough to be a real romantic (e.g., enjoys Broadway musicals, looking for a "soul mate," etc.), you should try to avoid this person at all costs. She will eventually end the relationship because she ultimately comes to believe she deserves so much better than you. These so-called romantics then proceed to reenact this scenario over again and again, trying to find their non-existent "soul mate," their perfect match in the world. In reality, they are frantically searching for a man who will carry on their idealized projection. Men who are willing to do this are essentially live organ donors for women who need heart transplants. All of us would be better off if we forgot this "soul mate" crap.

Worse yet, a romantic doesn't leave you but stays and devotes the rest of her life to finding fault with you or, even worse, makes you a home improvement project. You have seen these guys. Their wives are always telling them to sit up straight, not talk with their mouths full and have a list of chores for them to do. They are no longer able to figure out how to buy clothes and have to take their wives along with them for approval. Which basically makes them the gofer on a construction site.

So you want us to tell you the early warning signs? There is no point in it but we will anyhow, just for the satisfaction of saying we told you so. Basically, the more insecure you are the greater the likelihood you will fall deeply in love and your symptomatology will have psychotic overtones, for which there is no medication except large doses of reality. In this mode of so-called love, your sense of reality becomes distorted, you become euphoric one moment and despondent another. One day you are crazy with jealousy, the next day you are ecstatically focused on your time together. You are convinced you can't live without her. Every time you are apart you are like a junkie in withdrawal. You need a fix, and you don't ever want the craving to go away. You have physical symptoms: heart palpitations, elevated blood pressure, butterflies in the stomach, dizziness, loss of appetite and sleep, you are unable to concentrate at work, and your mind always wanders to her. Unbelievably you're not interested in other women. (This last symptom really begins to concern your BAD Dude friends.)

You have probably seen those young couples embracing each other in the parking lot of the grocery store on a spring afternoon. He has one hand on her ass and the other on her breast, and their tongues are down each other's throat. People are walking by and staring. She is trying to crawl up the side of his leg and her dress rises above her panties, and she doesn't care who sees. Dogs bark at them and sniff their crotches. They can't stop themselves and don't care who is watching. Even as you are driving away they are still at it, and you can't stop checking out her ass out of the corner of your eye. Once that had been you. Now you are embarrassed and find yourself melancholy for the rest of the afternoon.

Couples in this altered state of consciousness often decide to marry and have children, at worst they have hot sex. The point is, this is not love. The shaking out of this reality can take up to three to seven years for most couples. Researchers who have measured the bio-chemical basis for the duration of romantic love, from that first moment of intense infatuation until one feels completely neutral, found the average hormonal peak was between 18 and 36 months. It is not surprising divorces peak between 4-7 years. (And you just thought the two of you were unhappy.)

Never Say "I Love You"

. . . **in a tender, caring moment** (even if she washes your car).

. . . **in a passionate, erotic moment** (unless she cums first and tells you to knock it off so she can get some sleep).

. . . **if she turns sullen and tearful** (after having discovered another woman's panties, barrette or wet spots on your sheets).

. . . **after she says "I love you" and expects to hear it in return** (and you're still fantasizing about her idiot savant sister).

. . . **to get sex or money** (unless you really need it).

. . . **to resolve a fight** (except when you are wrong on every account and have been a real asshole. You are safe there).

. . . **as a desperate tactic to keep the relationship together** (until the holidays are over and you can find someone else and dump her first).

. . . **when you are wasted on drugs and alcohol** (well beyond pain and 0.2 and your autonomic nervous system is shutting down. In which case you are not responsible).

. . . **when you are shit-faced stupid in love** (and think God's talking to you through your erection).

. . . **when you are desperate, lonely, unhappy and contemplating suicide** (this is not a good time for reality).

. . . **so that she will immediately take off her clothes and massage you in warm oils, while her two teenage girlfriends make love to you**—(Oh hell! Every rule has its exception).

. . . **because it will make you feel like a nice person** (someone she could admire and respect, someone worthy of her carnal knowledge—come on, who are we kidding? Don't do it).

LOVE 6. You Deserve Love—Sucker. The BAD Dudes are going to share something very frightening with you. If you are the sensitive or squeamish type, stop reading now! If you think of yourself as a romantic or idealist—Stop! Now! If you flunked the "Are You Gender Challenged?" test at the back of this book—Stop! Do not read any further. You have been warned and we will not take any further responsibility. If you are a "Relationships Parolee" and want to go back in and serve time—then this is for you. If you are the unrequited type and have left a trail of relationship destruction—read on. If you see yourself as a "nice guy" that women just never seem interested in— keep reading.

It is clear that nature has done a better job in figuring out how to get us interested than in keeping us together. (And you thought that you just fell in love.) You not only don't have a clue, there is nothing you can even do about it. The first thing you have to do is give us a break about you and her being so special. Intense, passionate love, deeply heartfelt love, is as common and predictable as having to piss when you wake up in the morning. Nature is simply playing games with you.

"What is this game?" you ask. The chaos all about us, that's what this game is. The karmic pain of having to confront the loneliness of relationships breaking up and then having to start over with someone new and then break up again—doing it over and over. The anguish and pain of infidelities, the jealous tirades of being cheated on, two-timed, cuckolded, dumped for some else—different, newer, better. The flirtation with and seduction of the innocent, lusting after the girl next door and the intruding fantasies of other women as you screw your new girlfriend. What about the furtive lunches, secret affairs and illicit

124

motel rendezvous? The constant and insatiable wanting of someone new and different, and the chronic dissatisfaction with the woman you are with, all of which eventually give way to unrequited longing and bitter disillusionment—the sheer scale of it all is staggering. That's pretty much the way it's supposed to be. Don't let all the moralists running around shouting it's the end of the world shame you into believing differently. The fact that it is painful and destructive doesn't change anything. Go ahead fall into glorious love and start the cycle of chaos all over again. See if anyone really cares. Let the games begin!

LOVE 7. Is There Anything Beyond The Games? Of course there is. However, this is only for the most hardened relationship veterans. Really BAD Dudes who have been through the sexual wars, have been seriously wounded, who have stared into the jaws of love and not blinked. This is only for men who meet the standards of the Order of BAD Dudes—the relationship amputees, the post-sex syndromed, the haggard men who stare off distantly and who look older than their years, the ones who dive to the ground when startled by a friendly woman or wake up screaming with night sweats because they are living with one.

Most relationships are wars about how the other person doesn't or can't meet your needs. Your partner or spouse is not capable of loving you unconditionally. That is their unforgivable flaw. When you grow up you understand this and don't expect it. The relationship starts as a romantic delusion, sexually hot, becomes a struggle over control and boundary issues, and ends in resignation and despair. The only important question is, what do you do next? All relationships end. Some end in divorce, some by death (sometimes under suspicious circumstances), and others by giving up or by riding it out. All end painfully. What else is there to know?

It is estimated that 5 out of 10 marriages end in divorce, and that 3 of the 5 remaining marriages are unhappy relationships. Those two remaining relationships don't have "love," rather they have *relationship wisdom.* They have moved past the need for romantic love or being in love or falling in love. They have come to embrace the limits of what they can put up with from each other, especially during the hard times. This entails qualities such as respect, tolerance and compromise—the really impossible things to give to someone you love.

The fact is, our distorted notions of romantic love are almost always crushed by our early twenties and are perceived as hollow and fraudulent, leaving many if not most of us cynical, and even more, distrusting. We don't find our soul mate and we don't live happily ever after, and there is no goddamn tooth fairy either. If you are lucky, love is seen for the foolish and destructive act it is.

Sometimes we settle for lust or security or companion-ship. Maybe we just want to make sure we get enough sex before we die. Or perhaps we just want to fit in with everyone else—you know, have a purpose, a role and a place, and not have to be so lonely all the time. We want to meet someone who will make us feel better about ourselves, someone to lean on, and not have to do everything by ourselves. Sharing the inside of one's life with someone else wards off the pain of our separateness. Hell, even fighting is better than being alone.

The real struggle in life begins when we make these compromises without giving up our delusion that there is real love out there waiting for us. This is like watching the menacing death throes of a Great White hooked on bated chum. It thrashes like hell, but it dies.

Revelation #3: Debriefing

Warning! You're Entering A Bio-Hazard Zone

Proceed with caution. What we are about to share with you next is the most explosive and really ugly thing we can tell you. We hope we have your trust by now. Okay, proceed: Successful relationships don't have very much sex either. Sex isn't that important to a good relationship and, in fact, may even be contraindicated. Those who are unable to give up sex and seek relationship wisdom will be among the 80 percent who will always move away from a relationship because they feel the disappointment, the sense that there is more. Your choice.

Is there anything beyond hopeless resignation, you ask? The answer is yes, but not much. However, what we are about to reveal here comes from the mystical knowledge of the Order of BAD Dudes. Only those who have fully paid their membership dues should keep reading. This requires embracing your resignation and loving it rather than your partner. Say what?! Yes, you must move beyond all your previously accepted notions of what love and despair are.

You must give up believing anyone who says you need to change your consciousness and wants to charge you a fee in order to help you find love—you don't need to do anything. In fact, the less the better. Most of us have been trying too hard at too many things most of our lives. You don't earn love as if it were a promotion or a reward for good behavior. It is not bestowed on the most worthy or successful. In our "Can Do" culture it has to come as a big disappointment to find out you can't work on love in your spare time. There are no workshops, community college classes or PBS gurus who can help you remake yourself on a weekend, no books that can guide you to it, therapy can't do it for you, even spending a lifetime working on your own growth and personal development won't help you find love (love many pets routinely receive).

This stuff is not a goal or something you achieve or accomplish, you can't possess it, it is nonmaterial, and is all about us in the way the air encloses us. Unfortunately most of us are unable to experience it when it is given to us. For a long time we are too busy with our lives and with lust, and then we become too frantic in our search for it. The real lovers, wasted like burned out addicts, have been clean for a long time now, having given up their romantic fantasies of the relationship. Over the course of a long relationship love is produced, it is a byproduct, the same way excrement is produced by the body when it is fed. You have to start looking in the compost—that's where it's at.

Revelation #4:
Advanced Relationships

*"Relationships Are A System Of
Self-Organized Criticality"
And So Is Everything Else*

Sunday evening we are invited over to a friend's home by his friends, minister, wife and children, for dinner and an "intervention" for his alcohol problem. We sneak out to the garage and knock down long-necked Coronas. Later, while watching Masterpiece Theater, we take turns trying to hit on his wife. After the news and bouts of shits and shakes, the police ask us to leave. We swear off being *chemically inconvenienced* and head over to the Sex-A-Rama/Auto Parts Emporium to celebrate our first day of sobriety. We hope to cure our one-eyed dog's astigmatism by getting them petted. Since they wouldn't sit up and bark at the topless bar, we blow a roll of quarters on the sex arcade, watching dwarf quads have sex and then get tossed. We end up discussing "Queuing Theory" at an acute inpatient detox center.

Relationship: *A system of self-organized criticality made up of many similar, interacting components that don't settle down to a stable configuration, but rather push them-selves to the verge of instability.*

In other words, aside from describing an episode of diarrhea, this means relationships, by definition, are screwed up, just as you have always suspected.

Chaos Theory probably provides the most parsimonious definition of the relationship between men and women. It may, indeed, be all there is to know about everything. Your life-long struggle to locate what little order there is within chaos, to find the subtlest basis for any principles underlying male-female relationships, will probably go unrewarded. In fact, you must confront why you want to gain this understanding. It will not help you get a date, get laid or have a successful relationship. It will probably even get in the way of any of these possibilities. This is especially true if you try explaining your actions or reasons to any woman in these terms. In fact, you would be best advised to keep this information to yourself at all times and never tell anyone what you have read here.

Relationships—A Rotisserie League For Gangsta Women

As a BAD Dude who gets involved with a woman you are all alone, pitted against a team of women who are licensed relationship experts (L.R.E.). They have attended innumerable seminars and workshops on relationships, read every issue of *Cosmopolitan* and *Woman's Day*, and hundreds of bodice-ripping romances. They have spent a lifetime perusing the self-help section of bookstores, including every book on what is wrong with men (and there are hundreds). These women have many years of therapy among them. Chances are, one or more of them is a therapist. In addition, they have a sophisticated comparative database of enormous proportions derived from TV soaps and talk shows with which to evaluate your demographics and personality. There are any number of available personality profiles (Meyers-Briggs, the Ennea-gram) to measure just how dysfunctional or potentially disturbed your "type" really is. Furthermore, they are constantly networking (i.e., mainframing) over lunches, dinners, and coffee, etc., to initiate three key activities as outlined below. The BAD Dudes put this book together to help balance the equation in relationship negotiations—and it is a negotiation, never forget that.

PHASE I. Embarrass You Into Hiding

Women. A survey taken for a woman's magazine found that 74 percent of women tell their friends intimate details about their sex lives. This is a confessional process in which the woman you are dating reveals all of your faults to all of her unhappy, jealous and man-hating friends: the hair dresser who just caught her boyfriend cheating; the understanding store clerk who was just beaten by her husband; and the butch bank teller who keeps hitting on her, etc. You get the picture. She needs reassurance and will seek it just about anywhere or with anyone who can be objective about her situation.

She will tell them the size of your dick and if you come prematurely, how much attention you pay to her body orifices, to her sister's orifices and to sports on TV. There will be discussions of your DMV, credit and prison records, tattoos, large unexplained scars and peculiar habits with bodily processes and effluents. They will hear how you are always bringing up old girlfriends and keep a tire iron under the front seat of the car. They are taken aback by how little you make and how insecure and jealous you really are of her.

BAD Dude. When you get together with your one friend, for three hours on Monday night to watch football, you will tell him she has nice tits and you like her. He will want to know if she goes down on you yet, and does she have any good-looking girl friends.

PHASE 2.   She Admits You're A Loser

Women. This second phase of mainframing requires ruthless interrogation of her by those who say they care and love her the most. All those people who are so happy for her will soon engage in unprovoked attacks on her character, motives and judgment, seeking to exploit her every vulnerability. For months she will have to justify how she could possibly be interested in someone as dubious as you, which is a measure of just how insecure and inadequate she must really be. Her friends will question how she could give up one minute of time with them in order to be with you. If she continues to see you they may reject her friendship. She'll be shamed into believing that she did something wrong because she has a life now and can't get together at their convenience any longer.

Her smiling family, who want nothing but the best for their little girl, begins to undermine her confidence in the relationship. They begin by withdrawing emotional support from her and initiating a campaign of nagging doubt about your character. If the relationship becomes serious enough it will culminate in their charging you with kidnapping their daughter and forcing them to hire a deprogrammer and a private detective who will find damning evidence that you don't like her family. They will all try to convince her to leave you and return home where they can better control and manipulate her. You should not be intimidated by this process. It is normal. In some indigenous cultures they have a ritualized kidnapping to symbolize the grief of the family's loss. However, the next day they have a celebration to acknowledge their daughter's new beginning. But then they are considerably more civilized than we are.

BAD Dude. As the relationship with a woman intensifies, you will stop seeing your one friend (whom you had suspected all along), but for now will continue playing golf with that jerk at work. Your family won't have a clue as to what is going on with you.

PHASE 3. Hardballing The Relationship

Women. If you have dated over a year, your girlfriend will begin to pull together a hardened team of relationship veterans (embittered single and gender-disoriented women), to begin serious negotiations to determine if you are serious. Her mother will be the team captain, brought in to hardball you like the closer at a high-volume used car dealership.

BAD Dude. We want you to know that the Order of BAD Dudes has got your back covered, but at a safe distance. You essentially have three choices at this stage of the relationship:

1. You can reject the relationship and die a lonely death on a Saturday afternoon, in a beer delirium, while watching a Sports Channel Southeast Conference Football game, with *Debbie Does Dallas* in your picture-within-a-picture function, while engaging in the classic "repetitive motion syndrome." As you slump there the polyps up your ass are racing your metastasizing prostate and fist-tight aorta to determine which will be the first to shut down a vital sign before you ejaculate. We suggest you drain the lizard faster.

2. You can get trapped into trying to prove you are not an asshole like all the other men in her life. You know: reform yourself, become a better man for her. This is an unworkable strategy that you should leave to a better man than yourself. Watching relationships like this is similar to ordering the *Time-Life Video Trials of Nature* (about the

cruelty of animals in nature) with close-ups of a great white shark (her) biting the head off a seal pup (you).

3. Lastly, you can passively go along with the program and keep saying, "Yes, Dear . . ." hoping she doesn't catch on to you. She gets to decide everything. Any questions?! Let's be clear here, you are not the lead dog on this sled run and are not going to like what you smell for the next 500 miles.

Attitude Adjuster: *However, there is one last option we reluctantly share with you: You can bullshit her. Show no fear—explain to her how you were framed for the violent felony conviction; how it was an accident you got caught embezzling and had to file for bankruptcy but were able to settle with the IRS; that you are nearly off the penicillin and have been promised a promotion down at the car wash next summer; that your ex-wife left you and took the kids because you hit her one time, just a little, and, besides, the insurance paid everything off and you made your own bail—she will believe all of this and more, so long as you can convince her that you are full of potential and that with her help you could turn it around again—"The MAN is in the house!"*

Transforming A Polygamous Carnivore Into A Monogamous Herbivore

A wealth of data examining human sexuality consistently suggests that the human male is in all probability biologically driven to mate with multiple females and is not monogamous by nature, something a BAD Dude innately understands. The aberration of pair bonding (marriage and shacking up) among Homo sapiens, as compared to 90 percent of all other species, is likely the result of culturally imposed imperatives based on a number of factors: economics (the couple as a more cost effective social unit); contemporary cultural notions regarding romantic love; a means by which to assure social order (e.g., identify paternity, inheritance, property rights, etc.); a basis for controlling sexually transmitted diseases; and as a solution to conflicts resulting from males competing for sexual access.

As a man this means that once you marry you will come into conflict with your own nature. It is the sacrifice men make for the security of a relationship. Chances are, you will soon have to give up sex, much like that listless silverback male gorilla you see sitting in captivity at the Wild Animal Park, playing with itself and eating its feces as it vacantly stares back at you.

The two primary stimuli to male sexuality and arousal are: 1) the quest for sexual access (i.e., the chase) and 2) the seeking of sexual variety. When there is no chase or variety there is very little sex (try explaining this to your wife or girlfriend). This does, however, explain why extra-marital affairs have always been predominantly by men. Particularly by successful men.

A number of studies have shown that the more successful a man is the more likely he is to have an affair. He is able to achieve all the benefits of a stable mono-gamous relationship, plus continuous sexual stimulus. Economics apparently force the lower status male to remain faithful, unwilling to risk a divorce and the subsequent economic disaster that it might entail. This same pattern is now emerging among women who have become successful and dominant in the marketplace, and by lesbian woman who play the masculine or dominant role in the relationship.

Many cultures, at different times in their history, have understood all this and have institutionally provided for it. In Europe during the 17th century a gentleman would have a wife to bear him children and manage his estate, a well-to-do woman friend to be seen in public with, and a courtesan for his sexual pleasure. This seems most civilized. (However, most of them also died of syphilis.) Today, as a man, you have few choices, but they are yours to make:

A Short List Of Relationship Options

- Marry and be put out to pasture as a sexually castrated herbivore, or worse yet develop a taste for plain *vanilla* sex.

- Marry and have affairs, if you think you can afford them. Remember you can only divide your property in half so many times, until you will be forced to live with a woman or in poverty or both.

- Have serial marriages or relationships. (A particularly popular and expensive front-load strategy by middle and upper classes.) However, it assures that life doesn't pass you by.

- Become a misanthrope and forgo all relationships. This is probably the most sane alternative, but then who ever argued the human species was sane? In a paean to sanity, many indigenous cultures were very advanced compared to ours and maintained separate lodges, so that men and women did not reside together.

Attitude Adjuster: *The truth is, serial monogamy is really about dominant Bad Dudes getting extra sexual resources (i.e., women). This is not unlike being a freshman in high school and having a senior come along and take your desert. These alpha Dudes monopolize the reproductive years of many women, thereby depriving less dominant men of mates and children. What can we tell you, it is better to be near the front of the line in the gang-bang of life.*

Castrated And Married Men Live Longer Than Single Men!

As a reasonable BAD Dude you have probably asked yourself from time to time, why do eunuchs and married men outlive single men? Or, is there any difference between getting married and having your balls cut off? The answer to this latter questions is—no. Both eunuchs and married men outlive single men by an average of six years.

Research on nematodes (*Caenorhabditus elegans*) showed that producing sperm significantly reduces the male worm's life span by fifty percent. The researchers considered this a challenge to the *cheap sperm, expensive egg theory*. It also provides some explanation for the longer life expectancy of castrated males.

Let's see if we have got this straight. You sold the Harley, stopped hunting wild pigs, spelunking, hang gliding, white water rafting, ocean kayaking, mountain climbing and bungee jumping—and now they are saying your nads are killing you and that the only antidote is marriage or castration! This raises the next obvious questions.

Why does marriage extend life? And is it worth it? Surveys consistently show that single persons (i.e., never married, divorced, separated or widowed) are not as happy or satisfied with their lives as married couples. They have more health problems and depression. These surveys also show that a higher percentage of married people survive cancer at nearly every age, and that marriage is associated with a five year increase in survival length. The good news is that single persons will die sooner anyway and be put out of their misery. If you are single, don't want to get married, and this depresses you even more, you can always get your voice raised an octave and live six more miserable years longer as a contralto. Send for our BAD Dudes' "Home Castration Kit" now.

For singles the highs are higher and the lows are lower, with generally more lows than highs. Still, surveys of married couples show they envy the freedom of single life. You can't win. Regardless of where the grass is greener, married couples metastasize more slowly in front of the TV set than single individuals out networking and working out.

There are really two competing theories here: 1) One argument is that generally healthier people get married and that most of the rest are not really single by choice, despite what they say. This can be referred to as the *Slag Theory* of the downward spiraling misfortunes of the chronically single into an undifferentiated nonreproducing gulag. 2) The second argument is that singles don't really die earlier—they just live more life in a shorter period of time. Hapgood in his book *Why Males Exist* makes the case for those who die sooner. His research, on males across all species, suggested that ". . . any male who tried to live a sober, sensible, careful life might live a long time but he would never reproduce." The reckless ones may live a shorter life but it is a fuller life. He further notes that sex makes males of all species do stupid things.

But, you ask, what has all this got to do with having balls? Researchers who weighed the testicles of primates (there's a hell of a job) found a relationship between testes weight in comparison to body weight. Primates with high "relative testes weight" tended to be more polygamous.

Key to this development is the sexual promiscuity of the female. If there's a good chance she is fooling around, you need a high sperm count. Human males fall in the middle when it comes to testes weight. This suggests two things: 1) You're programmed to fool around and not be monogamous, and so is the woman you are involved with. 2) You are trying to assure your genes are passed on and she is trying to make sure she invests in the best genes possible.

Attitude Adjuster: *Your choice, you can live longer or you can live fuller, but you can't live longer _and_ fuller. Don't wimp out on us now—go for it!*

A 50-Year Relationship Or Five 10-Year Relationships. It's All The Same!

Two Arrows of Time in the Assumptive Masculine Reality

1.→
Objective Time
438,000 hrs.
18,250 days
2,600 wks.
600 mos.

←2.
Subjective Time
A long goddamn
time

Sleep
[16.7 yrs. (33.4%)]

Work
[12.8 yrs. (25.6%)]

Watching TV
[8.4 yrs. (16.7%)]

Driving
[4.2 yrs. (8.3%)]

Misc. Time Apart
[3.5 yrs. (7.0%)]

Talking
[3.5 yrs. (7.0%)]

You Have Completely Forgotten and Can't Remember Anything

**Really ugly, unpleasant
tension-filled time
together**
[3.5 yrs. (7.0%)]

1% --------- 6 months of wonderful, --------- 1%
pleasurable time together

------------- 20 hours of hot sex ----------------
.0000456%

Having Sex With Hundreds Of Beautiful, Sexy Women

Think about this for a moment. Make a short list of the studs in pasture of our time—Beatty, Presley, Sinatra, Jagger, Nicholson. In the vernacular of inner-city streets, "these dudes have poked more holes" than a rental backhoe with a posthole digger. Between them they might acknowledge 7-8 children. Wilt Chamberlain claims to have had sex with 20,000 women, and he has no children. Meanwhile, down the street from you is a paunchy, balding, retired pipe fitter who has been married 27 years to the same woman, the only person he has ever had sex with, and he has eight. In a society in which bumper stickers on "Beemers" proclaim "He who dies with the most toys, wins!", who do you think will have made the greatest evolutionary impact? Compared to Warren Beatty this old fart is the Emperor Moulay Ismael the Blood-thirsty of Morocco (who sired 888 children) of his time.

You don't need to look any further than an analysis of electronic communications systems in order to understand how the pipe fitter outfoxed all the sexual studs. *Braess's Paradox* states—"increased capacity in congested electronic networks slows down communication." How's that again, you ask? By maximizing choice (i.e., self-interest) in noncooperative games everyone may be worse off. What?!

If you have financial independence and sexual choice as these have evolved in our society, then you will probably choose ontogeny over progeny, i.e., self-development and self-interest over having children as a biological and economic strategy. You will screw around more but have fewer children.

As the GNP of a nation rises, the birthrate falls. Individuals and couples of high SES (socio-economic status) have fewer children, more stable marriages, and more sexual affairs. When times are good, the well-off choose a strategy of putting their eggs in one basket. The poor in our country have many children because it is a good economic strategy, while the middle-class have to struggle to figure out how it can afford even one or two. Obviously, something has gone wrong when the most advantaged of a culture choose *not* to have the most children. In fact, history is little more than a chronology of how the wealthy have bred themselves into insanity and extinction.

If you watch the celebrity culture of the successful (the ones with the most financial and sexual choices), you will see that they seldom settle down and commit to relationships, have fewer children, and because of busy careers have no time to raise them even if they have them. They keep changing partners and are disappearing little by little. Arguably, their extinction from the gene pool is good for society in the long run. Still they leave behind a few excessively ambitious and untalented progeny who persist in aspiring to singing, acting and/or political careers and celebrity status of their own. This has resulted in a social class of whining brats who do obscene things to get our attention, including writing books trashing their parents. Are you listening?

So you want a new car, a nice home, the ability to travel, an interesting career, a nice wardrobe, a comfortable retirement. So you will put off having children or have few or no children—this is our individual and collective narcissism in the age of consent. Children are expensive and time demanding. This is ontogeny, this is having choice, this is the pursuit of life, liberty, and self-interest.

Attitude Adjuster: *The BAD Dudes would just like to note that in the end (not that it matters much) you will probably find you have enjoyed your entire life having made the wrong choices—for yourself and everybody else, forever. Oh well, its probably too late now anyhow, so don't feel bad.*

The Collapse Of Relationships Due To Declining Marginal Returns

Simple Version

1. Human societies are problem solving organizations.

2. Sociopolitical systems require energy for maintenance.

3. Investment in sociopolitical complexity is a problem-solving response. Increased complexity requires increased cost per capita.

4. Sociopolitical organizations encounter problems that require increased investment to preserve the status quo.

5. The need for increased complexity must be met by more costly responses, as the cost of organizational solutions grow.

6. A point is reached at which continued investment does not give a proportionate yield, and marginal returns begin to decline.

7. As stresses inevitably arise, new organizational and economic solutions must be developed, typically at increasing costs and declining returns.

Complex Version

1. You ask her out in the hope of getting laid.

2. It seems cheaper to move in together than to keep dating: besides, the sex is great.

3. She says she is leaving if you can't commit . . . so what the heck—you marry her.

4. The two of you decide to buy a house with a thirty year mortgage. You can have the dog you wanted.

5. You have taken a second job and she is pregnant with a second child. You are fairly certain the child is yours.

6. You begin to wonder why the hell you are in this relationship—there is no sex, she constantly nags you and you have no money of your own.

7. You and your wife are in couples and financial therapy. Your kids see their own counselor. Your girlfriend gained 50 lbs., but your dog still loves you.

8. As marginal returns on investment in complexity declines, a society invests more heavily in strategies that yield proportionately less.

9. Excess productive capacity and surpluses are allocated to current operating needs. When a major stress surges there are little or no reserves to cope with it.

10. Investment in complexity is increasingly an unattractive strategy, when a population is receiving little return on the cost of supporting complexity.

11. The loss of complexity brings economic and administrative failure. This is an economizing process in which collapse may be the most appropriate response. Such societies have not failed to adapt. In an economic sense they have adapted well. For those who value civilization, perhaps not as well as they would have wished.

—J. Tainto,
The Collapse of Complex Societies

8. Your wife is now working full-time. You are a two income family struggling to make it. You have no savings and she is pregnant again.

9. The two of you stopped fighting and no longer talk to one another. She has lost interest in "Dead" concerts and has started farting out loud. The variable interest on the refinance is burying you.

10. You come home to find the locks changed. Her attorney serves you divorce papers. She continues to date him. You get to see the kids on weekends if she is more pissed at them than at you.

11. Your girlfriend left. Your home and half your income go to spousal and child support. You are on unemployment and in contempt of court; you see a probation officer once a month for threats you made to your wife and boss; and you just met a woman who loves you—Q. Do you (a) start a new empire or (b) enjoy village life?

—The BAD Dudes,
Relationship Realities

It's Great To Be The King
(as in, who put that bitch on a throne?
and who made that bastard king?)

The correct answer is always, "I got up here with your help. Now, how do I get down without breaking my neck?" And . . . "No, I'm not giving you a turn!" It's a little like being rich and telling someone who is middle class or poor that the personal costs of being rich are too high. They won't believe you and will want to find out for themselves—that is the state of relationships today. Men and women want "safe" relationships, relationships in which they feel in complete control and without risk. They want to be on top, or childless, or single because they can no longer trust, and who's to say there is much to trust in this day and age?

In his book, *Denial of Death*, Ernest Becker (with an intellectual assist from Otto Rank), sets forth key psychological dynamics in human relationships—the negotiation of power. The premises are quite simple:

- **All relationships are unequal by nature** (this is despite Constitutional guarantees);

- **Because of this inequality one person has more power than the other** (i.e., money, education, intelligence, beauty, personality, etc.);

- **A relationship is often formed around this unstated inequality** (enabling, co-dependency, enmeshment, love);

- **The party that has been coronated is made to feel powerful and omnipotent.** (It's great to be the king for those who have never experienced it. But inevitably you are poisoned, stabbed or beheaded).

In time the more equal partner will come to resent the dead weight their dependent spouse, peasant or lover represents, and see him or her as not worthy. How many times have you have seen this improvisational theater at dinner parties? The couple from hell who needs an audience to talk about—why he married such an ugly woman, his impotence, her flatulence, his incontinence. *She* will try to screw the host tonight, because *he* is knocking up her younger sister. They play out this sequel to *Who's Afraid of Virginia Woolf?* for any willing audience.

The more equal partners (lord and master) can do one of two things: 1) see the emptiness of this solution, confront their own human imperfections, and resign as amicably as possible, or 2) find someone else they deem more worthy to worship them (A BAD Dude survey indicated that 9 out of 10 BAD Dudes preferred being worshipped to confronting their own emotional impoverishment). Popular traditional scenarios include a wife putting a husband through law or medical school, then his leaving her after having successfully established a practice; or, a young beautiful woman using an older wealthy man to establish an acting or modeling career—then dumping him.

- **The person who is "less equal", initially feels complete and safe in the world.** (At some indeterminate point in the relationship they will begin to hate your guts. They usually find a way to let you know.)

150

In time they will come to see how stupid, arrogant and incompetent their significant other is. Then they have two choices: 1) knock the self-important SOB on his or her ass, in order to salvage their own self-esteem, or 2) find someone more perfect, stronger and more powerful, and help them up onto a pedestal. Traditionally women have played out this enabler role, finding and remarrying child molesters, alcoholics and wife beaters. This is called re-enactment. There is one other "classic option" and that is to stay in the relationship and seek revenge over an entire life-time. We often celebrate this decision with silver and golden anniversaries.

This might be the wife who every day for forty-five years gets even, slowly, imperceptibly, always chipping away—she forgets the beer when she goes to the store; the eggs are always over or under cooked; she fakes her orgasm with increasing disinterest during perfunctory sex; you haven't seen your favorite dessert, rum bread pudding, for twenty years; she never hears what you say the first time, and never wants to do anything you do— day in and day out until you lie in a coma on life support, and she can't bring herself to unplug the respirator, but goes home on the day you die and enjoys cooking rum bread pudding.

- **Some couples, very few, have relationships in which the negotiation of power is continual.** (Don't worry. This does not mean you have to take turns tying each other up in order to get off)

151

Power is delegated to one or the other in different areas of the relationship, for a limited time, and as circumstances require. These are relationships that are emotionally healthy, and where trust has evolved. Each can see their own limitations and they love their spouses despite these limitations.

Attitude Adjuster: *Let's get real. A BAD Dude is no more likely to recognize healthy relationships than he would notice his spouse or girlfriend being abducted by aliens. In fact, the chances of her being abducted are greater than the two of you having a healthy relationship. Early in the morning a mysterious blinding light fills your bedroom, your significant other thrashes about until paralyzed and is transported to the mother ship by small gray, bug-like aliens. Hours later she is returned to the bed next to you and has no recollection of these events when she wakes up. You slept soundly. She has only the vague sense an object was implanted in her brain and a probe was inserted up her rectum, but other than that everything seems perfectly normal. You can't figure out why she thinks an object was implanted in her brain.*

A Commitment-Relationship-Type-Thing

This is probably as good as most BAD Dudes can do in expressing their interest in some form of relationship-type thing with a woman. Because expressions of feelings are difficult, we tend to avoid cliché euphemisms (e.g., "let's sleep together", "I love you", or "will you marry me"?) and resort to more precise and technical language. This is often accompanied by autonomic nervous system functions such as sweating, hyperventilation, farting, urinary tract urgency, and "counterfactual proposition-ing." However, a Dude's attempts at intimacy are fairly straightforward:

BAD Dude Straight Talk

Precise Statement No. 1—You suggest a mutual, prone compression of stroking interlocking lubricated ventral surfaces at variable compression and torque ratios, to achieve emission threshold (hopefully not prematurely).

Polite Euphemisms:

* Let's make love.
   or
* Let's strip down that old slant six I've got up on pulleys in the garage.

Precise Statement No. 2—A friend of yours suggests to his girlfriend that they enter into a cohabitational-strategy-type-thing, with a functional distribution of labor intensive modes, variable intimacy exchange, sharing cost ratio displacement in a vertically and horizontally fixed structural field.

Polite Euphemisms:

- Let's move in together!
    or
- Will you do janitorial work at my office on weekends?

Precise Statement No. 3—A desperate man asks a woman to enter into a joint investment venture with licensing agreement, option to franchise, go public, share tax and deduction schedules, and negotiate a Golden Parachute for both parties, in case a Black Knight comes along.

Polite Euphemisms:

- Will you marry me?
    or
- Will you loan me $20,000?

Precise Statement No. 4—Aw shit, I mean fuck it man, this is too god damnhard, it sucks, you know what I mean—don't look at me that way!

Polite Euphemisms:

- I love you.
    or
- Aw, shit. Fuck it!

Attitude Adjuster: *What more could we possibly add to "Aw, shit, fuck it!" This says it all—now here is an attitude! Let us all grovel at the feet of the master, bask in his light, redeem ourselves in his enlightenment. Learn to silently repeat this phrase under your breath as a personal mantra—join together with other BAD Dudes and take up this chant.*

Men Fabricate The Reality They Think Women Want

Put more simply, Bad Dudes lie to women almost all the time. We do it for their own good. We don't do it because we are pathological liars, but to avoid conflicts and to be seen as a person with socially acceptable thoughts, feelings and impulses (which is often not the case). We want to avoid hurting women by sharing our real thoughts and feelings (you know the ones we are talking about here). Anyway, we all know that women *want* us to lie to them. Which makes it easier to do. How many times have you played the game of—"Do you still love me as much?" or "Do you think I am as pretty as she is?" and most dangerous of all—"How do you like my hair?"—we suggest you go ahead and lie on this last one, even if you are trying to reform.

A BAD Dude isn't going to understand a woman unless he understands the power of talking, and specifically of words. We know what you are thinking—might as well pack it all in now and get put on a reservation in Nevada for men who can't communicate with women (hopefully it's the one with the bordellos). Research shows that on average a woman speaks 2,200 words per day and a man 1,250. More importantly, men's and women's brains are hardwired differently. Women have wider corpus callosums and talk more from their frontal lobes, with greater generalization of function in both hemispheres. Men talk more from their parietal region, with greater localization in one hemisphere. The end result is, women talk more, faster and about less than men.

Women believe in words in ways that men often don't fully comprehend or appreciate. They attribute magical powers to words, powers that will redeem them, make them feel safe and better about themselves. The phone is a mystical shamanistic totem of sacred and powerful forces by which women remain in psychic contact with the collective feminine consciousness. To a man it is simply the telecommunications component of a broad network of information systems, in which transmissions are sequenced in binary (0/1) code, yes or no.

Legions of women claim they feel unloved because their husband or boyfriend doesn't say the right words, but instead keeps trying to do something that will please her. No matter how hard he tries it is never enough. Nothing you do will prove you love a woman if you don't have the words. You can work hard your entire life, be a good provider, be faithful and considerate, but if you don't say special words, she will not be sure that you love her. As a result, a woman often feels betrayed by a man because he tries to tell her what he thinks she wants to hear.

The struggle, for a BAD Dude, is that we often don't feel the words women want. Rather, we feel hypocritical, manipulated or insincere in providing them. Many of us have withheld words women want to hear out of a sense of integrity and respect for a woman (these are the bravest of the BAD Dudes). We simply don't have the neurological hardwiring to make words as loquacious and sentient as required by women. This is not an issue that is going to resolve by telling men they have a problem and need to get into therapy in order to better express themselves emotionally. We will just end up having problems communicating with our therapists.

Most of the time we learn to keep our mouths shut rather than chance uttering the wrong words, which can have a devastating effect. We BAD Dudes would like to make the case that if women would stop emotionally interrogating us when we are trying to be objective, they would find us more forthcoming (this may be a tad optimistic). We quickly learn to shut up or lie. Please note that not saying anything doesn't work. You can speak in tongues, emit gastrointestinal noises or exhibit a variety of facial tic and spastic behaviors, but never say nothing.

Of course, lying and pretending is a strategy that ultimately fails. It starts as seduction during courtship, becomes appeasement over the course of the relationship, and finally it is used to hide our disappointments at the end. No wonder the truth appears so brutal in most relationships. This *frontload strategy* is often confabulated by BAD Dudes because we know that no matter what we say or do it will be discounted like a President's Day Sale at Nordstroms. Women want to know what we feel but with adjectives such as never, always, absolutely, deeply, truly, "the highest mountain," the deepest blue sea," etc. They want absolutes. But this will not be enough, it has to be with sincerity and real feeling. This leads to an upward spiraling inflation of the rhetoric between men and women that most men are unable to sustain.

Inevitably, words such as "almost," "most of the time," "probably" and the worst of all "I think I do" and "I am just trying to be honest" begin to creep into the certitude that women demand. The most successful men learn to inflate language to the limits of believability without lying, otherwise women won't believe you care about them.

Attitude Adjuster: *You are saying, how can talking be a problem? Isn't it the solution to most problems? Doesn't it separate the human species from other animal species? It is also what separates women from men. Talking can quickly overload a BAD Dude's central nervous system and quickly induce a wide range of symptoms, including: withdrawal, muteness, anger, ignoring or pretending to listen, turning up the TV, reading the newspaper, claiming a moratorium on talking because the news or sportscast is on, or the game is just about to start. He suggests "Let's talk later." Later he has a project he needs to finish or he's tired now and wants to go to bed. In the morning he is in a hurry to get to work early. The longer you can get away with this the longer the relationship will last.*

Relationships Are A Test About The Structure Of Reality That Men Can't Pass

It always begins as a relatively innocent and playful game, not unlike you and the Dudes playing a video game with 22 levels, and ends in your experiencing the perplexing and despairing conundrum that you will never know what it was all about (only got to level 10). This is as true on the first date, as after fifty years of marriage. Please note that for women the length of a relationship is a key biosocial marker demonstrating that time exists as a dimensional measure of reality. You will need to know this on the test, and watching Star Trek reruns won't help. The key question is as obvious as a fractal model of the chaos underlying the universe. She asks you one of the most important questions of modern theoretical physics today—*Is there an objective reality and can we know it?* However, she is subtle because she doesn't ask it straight out.

Depending on her theoretical school of orientation you may be asked: "What are you thinking?" or subtle variations on this theme. For example: "You seem very quiet and distant right now" or "Is something wrong?" Another school may rhetorically inquire: "Do you like how I had my hair done? It's important to keep in mind that the standard binary response of yes/no does not constitute a satisfactory mathematical proof, in her mind, that the two of you are sharing a binomial conversation, relation-ship or the same time-space continuum for that matter.

Perhaps one of the most subtle and difficult opening gambits entails her asking you, "Do you think I need to lose weight?" This will be followed by, "Exactly how much weight do you think I need to lose and how long have you felt this way?" The answer to this, in all likelihood, will remain an unsolved paradox among mathematicians and most men for many generations.

You still don't know it yet, but this is the beginning of a profound dialectical exploration of the basic forces, elements and dimensions of reality. You can make the time-honored but very dated mistake of being literal (see Newtonian Mechanics here). You tell her about the physical world as you observe it—you can't talk about your work because it is classified, but you can tell her that you've been laid off. You also share with her your interests in salt water aquariums, that her new haircut makes her look older (which you like), and that she is much heavier than when you met but that she carries the extra weight well, except perhaps on her hips. You continue on, obliquely, with all the many mundane and banal patterns of your thinking.

You operate with the theoretical insight that if you *really* told her your thoughts, for example, that you would like to buy an RV and travel around the country for ten years, or don't understand why she is so upset about your attempted unauthorized entry into her parallel port, that this would lead to a *paradigm shift*, confirming the underlying constancy of *Entropy* ($S = k \, \mathrm{Log} \, W$) in the universe. In practical terms, the fecal matter would hit the turbines for the two of you. It would get crazy and probably lead to a breakup of the relationship. Your emotional life, the weak attractional force in the relationship, would become squeezed tighter and tighter until the remnant core collapses into a gravitational abyss. You want to avoid this.

However, she sees the inherent contradiction in your assumptive model—that energy only transforms itself *(Law of Conservation of Mass-Energy)*. You can run but you can't hide. She is forcing you to deal with the more complex world of Quantum Physics—to look at the underlying subatomic particles of your relationship, to which you have no clue, and are trying to fake it. She is insisting on complex equations that see the smooth surface of the relationship as an illusion made up of many turbulent macro and micro elements. Key to the feminine assumptive reality is the *uncertainty principle*—she has her doubts about you.

You respond cleverly with the well tested paradigm of many years of experimental evidence—"I am not thinking about anything," or "Everything is fine, why do you ask?" You share with her the classical theory that the universe is comprised primarily of a Void or Nothingness. She, of course, automatically assumes that this was just a cleverly disguised metaphor for your relationship with her. You respond that you were just thinking out loud and didn't intend any such thing and that she is jumping to conclusions. She posits that there is a quivering motion that can't be accounted for, but has determined it's your heart, which is the only possible reason she continues in this dialog/relationship with you. However, it is still a *Cold Dark Matter (CDM)* that has to be resolved.

What you've secretly been wanting to tell her is your theory that relationships are a system of *self-organized criticality*. In other words relationships, by definition, are inherently unstable. This also explains your reluctance to commit.

She is thinking: I hope he doesn't cop out with some intellectualization to explain our relationship. Our relationship is all the metaphor he needs. While he is in his study or out in the garage searching for the subtlest basis for any principles underlying male-female relationships, I am cooking dinner and trying to pay the bills at the same time. If he wants some order, why doesn't he get off that computer and try picking up around the house sometime? Better yet, let's have a child.

Of course, she is not really asking you what *you* think at all. How many times have you fallen for this and tried to guess the right answer? She is not asking you about her hair, weight, your work, "queue theory" or what you think are the fundamental rules of the road governing interstate or galactic travel. She wants to discuss your cosmology on the origins of relationships and those basic structures underlying its reality (values, beliefs, feeling, intentions). This is feminine theoretical physics, the universe of the psyche.

She, too, is engaged in a constant experimental search for a *Grand Unifying Theory* (i.e., marriage) which would give a moral dimension to the *Big Bang* (see Einstein here, something about God not randomly pairing eggs and sperm). What she wants to know is how you feel about her and the relationship at this point in time. She is asking you about your *World of Deep Reality (WDR)*—do your theories on particles (words) and waves (feelings) collapse when rigorously tested? Put simply, do you love her or not and can you prove it?

For you, this is beginning to feel more like deep doo-doo than deep space. You are the Voyager space probe, now well beyond our solar system, having lost all contact with the command center at Huntsville. You just want to get back to e-mail hacking on an electronic bulletin board. You try to argue (but don't know it) that there is a knowable, objective reality—"Didn't I tell you last year that I loved you?" "Don't I wash your car and change the oil?" With that piercing-deeper-into-the-dark than most insight you offer, "Why would I be here if I didn't love you?" She argues, in a quiet voice you have never heard before, that there is a subjective *Strong Anthropic Principle (SAP)*. We not only create our reality but it exists in its entirety for our existence. You, on the other hand, envision a universe without *Strings* and suggest looking at this with *Fuzzy Logic*. She tells you that this is not theoretically possible no matter how much fuzzification you apply and, besides, this is a can of *Worm Holes* she doesn't want to get into.

Attitude Adjuster: *You flunked again. The BAD Dudes know how you feel. None of us have ever passed this advanced course in theoretical relationships either. But don't despair. We are filing a class action lawsuit alleging that this test is gender-biased and needs to be re-standardized so men can pass it at the same rate as women. Women are arguing that current standards need to be maintained and that dumbing down this test for men will only allow many clueless Dudes to believe they are actually engaged in a relationship. Our response is— so?!*

Inane And Banal Books On Relationships

As a sensitive BAD Dude you are weary of all the books about how men and women communicate differently from one another. These books suggest that men and women communicate at cross-purposes and with very different goals in mind. This notion has probably been around for a few thousand years, at least, and has led most of us to wonder if the opposite sex is of the same species or from a different planet. The sum of this nonsense seems to be that we BAD Dudes have a problem communicating with women, and need to change in order to facilitate healthier relationships, and not the other way around. Trust the BAD Dudes on this one, all the pseudo-meta-analyses of the state of relationships today doesn't have any clue as to what is going on.

The recent discovery by social scientists that men and women are different and that *form fits function* is hardly a revelation, but it does keep researchers off the streets and gainfully employed. However, if your girlfriend or wife has recently purchased a book on how men and women communicate and wants you to read it, humor her and pretend to read it. What the heck. If you can't communicate, what makes her think you can read? Just keep in mind that as long as she is making you the problem, this effort is a waste of time. The BAD Dudes say—*The differences between men and women extends beyond biology, is not a problem and doesn't require a solution.*

Please don't misunderstand us, regardless of your planet of origin. It has always been obvious to everyone that men and women communicate differently. So What?! How men and women communicate isn't the problem. If anything, we can't agree on what the problem is or even if there is a problem. Reducing the conflict between men and women to styles of communication is interesting in the same way research on genetic differences between men and women are interesting. However, there is nothing we can do about it and it has no practical value. Offering 2.7 billion men a weekend workshop on how to communicate better is not the answer, anymore than requiring all women to take a home repair course is.

To save you from being tortured by any more of these books and becoming even more confused—leaving you terrified that you can't say or do anything right—just keep in mind the two rules of communicating with a woman, which is basically all these books have to offer. Then be aware that these two rules are contributing to the craziness between men and women. Rather than being a supplicant to the neurosis of our times, be yourself. Learn to make constructive changes the way men have for generations before you, by pain and death.

First Rule Of Communicating

Listen to her, and acknowledge her feelings. Don't tell her she shouldn't feel that way, that she is overreacting, that it is no big deal, that she is imagining it, or that everything will be okay. Don't yell at her and tell her that she is crazy, paranoid, projecting, or needs to be medicated and/or institutionalized, and that she is just like her mother. Don't talk about her trust issues or the dysfunctional family she comes from. Don't tell her she needs a shrink and to stop getting advice about your relationship from her man hating friends.

Don't keep trying to convince her that you are not really like her father. No! Of course not, don't say any of these things. If you can't think of anything empathetic to say, say nothing, and simply hold her and be present with her in your silence, even if it is a bitter, angry, vitriolic attack on your character and integrity. You should not take this personally. Go ahead, pretend that her emotional world is the virtual world.

If you take this advice and say nothing but simply empathize, she will continue to get crazier and crazier as you support her distorted view of the world and of you. This will result in the creation of an emotional tyrant in your life, someone who will consume you and bend reality to fit her emotional needs, no matter how crazy and distorted they are. Remember, passivity breeds aggression. This is as true for a relationship as it was for Neville Chamberlain at Munich in 1938. You need to listen and empathize, and then assert your thoughts and feelings about things. Don't buy that crap that her emotional world is the true world (the Lebensraum or living space of your relationship) and that the rational world is the cause of all our problems.

Second Rule Of Communicating

When she expresses her feelings, don't try to make everything okay by helping her solve what you see as her problem. She is not asking you for a solution. She is asking you to understand and support her. You, of course, will not be able to do this.

This represents a great chasm in the world views of men and women. It is the difference between being and doing. If you don't act in the world she will have no interest in you, and will treat you contemptuously. She may not like the answer or solutions you offer, but it is not because she has a better answer to her chronic worrying about other people's feelings: that they won't like her, or will be mad at her, or will reject her, or be critical of her. There is the constant fear she won't do things well enough or the right or correct way. There is the chronic self-doubts and recriminations she feels, the sheer guilt and fear of being in the world. This creates a passive inertia that leaves her wallowing in worry, self-doubt and obsession that will explode on you when you suggest a solution. We suggest you keep offering solutions for your sanity and hers. The key is not to get mad when she always comes to you with her problem and doesn't take your advice or seem to have any faith in your years of experience in the world.

Attitude Adjuster: *As a BAD Dude you need to communicate your special needs as a man. Share how difficult it is to always be checking out the visual epigamic features of every woman who walks by, what it is like to be driven by a high-testes-to-body weight ratio,* *and that it's really difficult to stay interested in her sexually. Share with her the problems of testosterone and sexual dimorphism, how communicating is really difficult due to differing brain physiology, and that your visual-spacial abilities make you want to watch a ball game this Sunday, rather than visit her family. Give her a chance to listen and empathize for a change.*

Revelation #4: Debriefing

O-kaay! How long did it take you Dudes to figure out that almost all relationship guidelines are a total crock? Who are we kidding here? Using these guidelines, or any self-help books or audio or video tapes you have ordered from a TV infomercial, is like trying to comprehend your mortality by talking with an insurance agent. Your agent sits down with you to explain whole life versus term insurance policies, and then proceeds to tell you about the meaning of life with actuarial tables while quoting Martha Stewart and Kahlil Gibran.

Face it! You are going to go out there and screw up your own life in your own inimitable fashion regardless of what anyone suggests. You will inevitably choose the wrong person for a relationship, and then you will blame your dick or plead nolo contendere. Besides, you'll argue, how could anyone have foreseen the problems that would visit your relationship deus ex machina. "How could this have happened?" you will ask yourself over and over, and the answer is always the same every time. You will always minimize the negative contributions you make to the relationship's problems and exaggerate and blame her disproportionately. You will also argue, correctly, that if you applied all these guidelines, you would never find anyone who could have met them all. By these standards there is no right person, and everyone is dysfunctional. This is a wise observation.

You will always—repeat—always find someone you won't be able to get along with in a relationship. You'll never know why you can't get along with this person, or why you selected each other to be in relationship with. This is true no matter how "together" you are or how carefully you select. It is the human condition to live in denial, to rationalize away responsibility, and to minimize our faults. This is payback, nature's way. It's dharma. The smooth surface of the waters you see as your self are an illusion, but then, so is the turbulence of the relationship.

You may be saying to yourself, "They are wrong, the pain of my relationship is real." And so it is, but the turbulence is what keeps us from intimacy, from having to trust and depend emotionally on one another. It is what feels safe to us. You may be saying, not me, not us, we never fight or argue, we have a great relationship. These are the worst kind of relationships. They promote the illusion that there is no more to be done, that they are somehow above the fray and that relationships are not an "ordeal." They have chosen quietude above all else. They are the walking dead. Your only choice in a relationship is smooth or turbulent. Choose wisely, BAD Dude.

Revelation #5:
Reality Check

Relationships Are The "Joyful Participation In The Sorrows Of The World" (Upanishads)

We get tossed from detox for fighting among ourselves over a skinny 16 year old emancipated runaway who is trying to con the second year resident out of narcotics. One of us claims to be junkie, another a coke dealer, one a meth monster, an acid freak and a pothead. She says she is an undercover vice officer into aerobics and power foods. Monday, while out on bail, we join a fitness club (Titanium Buns) with aqua blue carpets and matching designer equipment—that's where the action's at. We knock back a few anabolic-amino-protein power shakes for carbo loading and hit on babes in sport bras who are into supersets and mass. Most of the time we just watch them work their hip adductors and ask insightful questions about their cardio routines and negative rep training. Our memberships are canceled for sniffing the seats of the women's exercise bikes. Really! You get a great endorphin rush from the warm plastic.

By now some of you are probably asking yourself—why bother? What's the point? These guys are obviously already having a great time without women. Why have any standards regarding women or expectations for a relationship? If you are desperate to have one, just marry the first woman who comes along—it's all apparently random and ultimately meaningless anyway. Isn't that what they're saying? How could someone possibly know who the right person for them is? Or if there is one or many right persons. How would you know them if you saw them? Is it even possible to meet them? Is the right person for you now, the same as the right person for you later? What if the right person(s) are already involved? Or you just missed them—they were just leaving as you got there? What if there is no right person? Some are just better for you than others? Maybe it doesn't matter who it is, so long as you care enough to stay involved and work it out. But, what if that isn't enough—how many times do you have to do it, can you do it, want to do it? You may ask yourself, after a while, why *do* I do it? This is good.

Why Do Men Turn Forty And Get Into S&M?

By middle age, BAD Dudes and everyone else are prone to becoming perverts, getting arrested, and being humiliated in front of all of friends, family and colleagues. This is true whether you are a former Chief Justice of the Supreme Court of New York who stalks the woman he is having an affair with or the president of an Ivy League university who makes obscene phone calls. We will just have to create a new Order of BAD Dudes to celebrate the perverts who go public. However, keep in mind that you are not a celebrity who could deal with it as an everyday occurrence, nor can you afford the Betty Ford Clinic or a ghost writer for an autobiography that would get you a spot on a talk show.

Perversion is a spiritual crisis, primarily of the middle-aged. It is a condition in which we come to believe that sex resides only in fantasy and no longer in our bodies, which have betrayed us. We create rituals and fetishes to protect ourselves and to once again feel in control, not unlike primitive men faced with an unknown world. Our unknown world is the inner-world. Couples who engage in serious sadomasochistic acts are seeking God. And all BAD Dudes know that freedom of worship is constitutionally protected.

So how do you go about recognizing whether you are in a spiritual crisis if you are not into S & M? Do you find yourself reading tabloid headlines in the supermarket checkout line and secretly enjoying them? Do you turn on smut TV (*Current Affair*, *Inside Edition* or *Hard Copy*) or worse yet, Reality TV, rather than watch the news first thing in the evening? Do you first open the newspaper to sensational journalism and gossip columnists? Are you among the depraved who watch TV talk shows? Or have you fallen among the most spiritually-bereft and enjoy spending all night on the Web trying to track down nude photos of Britney Spears? If this describes you, you are probably in denial and crisis.

Spiritual Crisis Indicator

[√] **Minister caught with prostitute!** He tried to save her many times with the help of your donations. Now God is asking you to send money to help save these women from *him*.

[√] **Married politician photographed with call girl!** Says she represented a political action committee (PAC) for disadvantaged young women trying to make ends meet. Claims all his constituents should have access, not just the powerful and wealthy with whom he is already having anal intercourse.

[√] **Doctor sexually molests patients under anesthesia!** Says these charges are prescription-induced delusions, and that he doesn't know how his Submariner Oyster Rolex got into her vagina, when he was only treating her ear infection.

[√] **Wealthy businessman discovered on a Internet child-sex ring floppy disk!** The defendant stated that he was seduced by all 42 runaways, who claimed to be 18-year olds.

[√] **Professional basketball player arrested by police officer posing as prostitute!** Wants to start a self-help program for athletes who are involved with groupies and prostitutes. He'd be happy to name players who don't have his stats, contracts, or playing time— and who haven't been arrested but should be.

[√] **Wealthy socialite couple (often in Florida) are divorcing and going public with all the sordid details as a legal strategy!** At the trial they accuse each other of bondage, failing to make the "A" social list, physical abuse, incest, homosexuality, transvestism, painting the statuary genitals in bright colors, swinging, sex with the servants and bad taste, but would like to reconcile for their children's sake.

[√] **Couple next door makes home sex films!** (a) You quickly check to see if you know them in the hope of obtaining a copy. (b) You threaten a law suit claiming they do not have a release or contract with you or your wife. (c) You buy your own video equipment and start producing/distributing your own films.

[√] **Desperate, middle-aged loser gets screwed-up younger woman (who has never seen or met him), to marry him on TV that night for a million dollars!** After the annulment she stated, "I did it on a lark." He said, "I was seeking true love." The BAD Dudes are shaking their collective heads in despair—a million is not going to be enough these days! We preferred seeing TV morning talkshow host Katie Couric getting her colon scoped.

Attitude Adjuster: *Forget all that Internet hype. We have the only __real__ nude photos of Britney. Log on at: www.BADDudes.com*

Old Dudes Doing Favors For Young Women

What is that special relationship between a mature BAD Dude and young woman? A study of 10,000 people in 32 countries found that, on the average, men were three years older that their mates. This is interesting but doesn't quite get to the heart of the matter. Leave it to the French to provide us with a wise Old World rule of thumb when it comes to this geezer-babe phenomenon. The French insist that the ideal age for the woman is half the man's age plus seven years $[M(a)/2+7=W(a)\geq18]$ (American specifications require that she must also be 18 years of age as well). This takes some of the fun and a great deal of the risk out of it. But it's a formula most Dudes could probably live with.

Yes! There is the possibility of life after death if you plan on being financially well-off in mid-to-late life. Otherwise you can stop fantasizing about a voluptuous younger woman. On the other hand, even a homely nurse-maid who bathes you and changes your bedpan three times a day may begin to look beautiful after awhile. Essentially everyone can play if they live long enough.

By age 35 there is an equal number of men and women in the United States. By age 60 there are 3.5 single women for each single man. On average, women live 7.8 years longer than men. In other words, we are dropping dead faster. However, for those of us who survive past 60, times couldn't be better to meet women. If you only have limited resources, you simply negotiate with a woman who has a lot less. This is a time-honored form of love called trading sex and companionship for resources. It doesn't really matter how much younger she is, only that she is over 18. Unless of course you are in Holland where the age of sexual consent is 12. There are so many men who still think they are in Holland. The BAD Dudes have listed all the pleasures of getting older and dating younger women— enjoy. And take good care of your health!

Why Old Dudes Date Young Women

- **Denial of Death.** A young woman with an older man is proof that there is life after death. You want to look into the metaphorical mirror and find youth.

- **Power and Status.** *Trophy wives* are a measure of your success. They are objects of beauty and power to be possessed. Your appreciation of art continues to grow over the years.

- **Character.** You have the strength of character to choose outer beauty over inner beauty—not mimic the moralisms of the herd.

- **Control.** You like feeling less challenged and threatened intellectually and emotionally. Besides, who wants to argue with a wife who is entitled to half your assets and pension?

- **Ego.** This feeds your vanity regarding your prowess as a male—you silverback stud, you.

- **Conquest.** The seduction and possession of a younger woman is challenging. You're a man of vision with boundless energy who needs new challenges.

- **Emotional Stasis.** This process offers you a way not to grow and change emotionally all the time. You have grown so much—you can give it a break occasionally.

- **Recapitulation.** You have earned a second chance to undo your early failures and to possess the women of your dreams. Now you can enjoy the youth you never misspent.

- **Less Demanding.** A young woman will never ask you to take ballroom dance lessons as a prelude to a two-day cruise from Long Beach, California to Ensenada, Mexico. A protracted and unending struggle with a woman wears you down after a while.

- **Ignorance is Bliss.** Younger women haven't been witness to twenty years of failure, screw-ups, and the gradual loss of your youth, which can be very unattractive. They also lack the contempt that comes with having to put up with you for so long.

- **Who Cares.** A 19-year-old can be extremely mature and find you "Like, totally awesome." They just can't seem to resist you. What's a guy to do? Besides, you have a car and can afford to eat at Burger King all the time.

- **Because You Can.** It's legal—everyone else can go screw themselves!

Trying To Achieve Orbit Velocity

The BAD Dudes believe it is important, when seeking out an aphrodisiac, that you are clear about what it is you really want. Do you want something that will make your Johnson instantly hard for a long time? Or, do you want a way to turn a woman on to you sexually, no matter how ugly, stupid, ignorant or crude you are? By differentiating your needs this way you can better understand if your problem is getting it up or scoring with women. Big difference. Hey, look! Don't you think if someone could sell a product that could do either of these that they would be the wealthiest person in the world and we would all know about it? This is just one-step-removed from penis enhancement surgery—that's where you mutilate your dick under the delusion that a half inch is the difference between inadequate self-consciousness and well-hung.

Why is the really good stuff always so secret and hard to get?—extract of tiger penis, powdered rhinoceros horn. Scoring Ecstacy at a rave party is amateur time. It's all just good marketing: find a market niche full of desperate people, offer false hope with empty promises, create a fraudulent product, make it difficult to obtain in order to jack up the price, then hope the FDA doesn't shut down your operation before you change names and addresses.

For BAD Dudes who feel a tad more desperate (and your concerns are no longer about meeting preestablished all-terrain performance objectives but getting it started and out of the garage) there's new hope. Urologists can now stick a needle in your dick and inject you with an anti-impotence drug, giving you a hard on for six hours at a time. Now there's a solution we've all been looking for!

180

Attitude Adjuster: *First off, the BAD Dudes suggest you forget anything you can purchase over-the-counter, get by prescription or that a friend will sell you. Don't believe anything a "junkie" or "coke head" tells you. The facts are, there is nothing you can chew, drink, snort, rub on, administer intravenously, or put in a body cavity, that will turn either of you on. There is no substance that will make your dick longer, wider, or harder, help you grow back hair on your head, stop graying or wrinkles, or make women desire you. However, there is stuff that will make your pee look funny, change your bowel habits, harden your stool, make your tongue dry and fuzzy, make you thirsty, dizzy, irritable or unable to sleep.*

How to Flatline Like A Gomer In A Coma

Man*: I am in trouble if she likes big dicks and doesn't think beer guts are cute. How long are we going to neck for? The torsion on my back is killing me and I have just sucked off 5 ounces of pancake make-up powder and can't swallow or pucker anymore. What does she really think about white Jockey shorts? What if I can't get her to come? For that matter, how do you ever really know if a woman comes? Damn, I think I am going to fart. Is there a discrete way to get a pubic hair out of your mouth? How do I explain I have condoms with me? I* think *my herpes lesions are completely healed. What if she takes this too seriously? Are we going to get liftoff tonight? Shit, we're up but for how long? Can we reach projected altitude, and maintain the required trajectory? What if the eagle can't land? Whoops! Don't have to worry about* *that—too bad we didn't reach orbit. I hope she doesn't want to talk all night afterwards.*

Woman: *Please don't let him be a techno-geek who treats sex like it was a NASA project. What if he thinks my breasts are too small or my nipples are too big or my vagina too wobbly? I don't want him to see my fat thighs, flabby butt and varicose veins. I hope it doesn't bother him that I want the lights off. Will I be too dry? Will he want oral or anal sex? Will I have an orgasm? What if I have more than one—Will he think I am too sexually aggressive? Is he just using me sexually or does he care about me? I should have showered. I wish I had put clean sheets on the bed. I don't think I can come because I have to pee so badly because of my bladder infection. I hope my period doesn't start. I hope he doesn't drool in my ear or put his tongue you know where and then try to kiss me. Should I tell him I don't want any hickeys? This just doesn't feel quite right, it's so dirty. I hope he doesn't roll over and fall asleep afterwards.*

Okay, we'll cut the crap, you want the technology without the philosophy. On the next page is the "Chart of Imaginary Erections." You should note that all of them are considered improper, immoral or are just plain illegal. More importantly, they are all available to just about everyone. However, you should use caution if you are not a Registered Aphrodisiac Technologist (RAT).

182

Chart of Imaginary Erections

Class	Effectiveness	Active Agent
Class I.	**Placebo Effect**	**Misc.:** vitamin E, oysters, Spanish fly (cantharides), powdered rhinoceros horn, synthesized pheromones, porcine musk, ginseng, cognitive enhancers (DMAE or Piracetam), herbal Ecstacy, guarana, ma haung; all balms, potions, creams, lotions, subliminal tapes, or CDs by Luther Vandross.
Class II.	**Mildly Effective**	**Disinhibitors:** alcohol, marijuana, opiates, tranks, hallucinogens (Only effective at moderate dosages. At high levels they can create impotency and unconsciousness). Roofies (GBL), GHB (gamma hydroxybutrate).
		Stimulators: caffeine, chocolate, cocaine, speed, yohimbe, damiana, schisandra, avena sativa, L-arginine, DHEA, saw palmetto and horny goat weed (Only effective in moderate doses. High usage results in agitation and incoherence.).
		Pharmaceuticals: Viagra and AndroGel.
		Fantasy & Pornography
Class III.	**Potent**	**Abstinence/Monogamy**
		Breaking Up (makes your Old Lady look good again)
		Forbidden-Illegal-Immoral-Dirty
		Delayed Gratification-Anticipation
		Dangerous-Exciting-Risk Taking
		Power Exchanges/Games
Class IV.	**Extremely Powerful**	**Conquest-Seduction**
		Young-Attractive-Charming (the second most powerful turn on for men)
		Power-Wealth-Success (the second best turn on for women)
		Impersonal-Detached-Uninvolved (aka the "zipperless fuck")
Class V.	**Lethal**	**New-Strange-Different-Exotic** (this is the most powerful aphrodisiac)

183

The Really Ugly Onanistic Wars

Everyone is pissing and moaning—what is wrong with relationships today?, as if *Ozzie and Harriet, Leave It to Beaver* and *The Brady Bunch* were some kind of golden age of relationships. Forget it. This is just the early sign of presenile dementia in another aging generation that can no longer remember how it really was. There never was nor will there ever be such an age. Some will argue that with all these divorces and single parent families something must be wrong—the only thing wrong is, we prefer it this way. Right now golden anniversaries don't rate that high on our lists of wants. This is despite the fact that just about everyone is looking for a stable relationship or changing one relationship for the hope of another. We can have stable, long-term relationships and families any time we want. Most of us reading this book just happen to live in a time and place where we can have many of our financial and emotional needs met *outside* an enduring relationship. This is a lot like that old saying, "Everyone wants to go to heaven, but no one wants to die." Everyone says they want a stable, long-term relationship; it's just that no one wants to die in one.

You want long-term monogamous relationships? Then you have to ask yourself what is destabilizing them. No, it is not drugs, alcohol, guns, pornography, welfare, TV or men. It is much more basic than that.

It means giving up interesting sexual partners for the rest of your life, not coming and going whenever you want or spending your money as you please, having to buy furniture that you don't like, not eating out when or where you want or watching whatever TV show or video rental your heart desires. It probably means living the rest of your life with someone you can't agree with about anything, such as who is going to shop for food, fix dinner, clean up, do the laundry, vacuum, mow the lawn, take the car in for repair? You endlessly debate who is the busiest and who is spending too much money. You feel tired, lonely, unhappy, asexual, listless, bored and depressed most of the time. This monotony is only broken by the heightened and chronic tension of conflict in the relationship. You don't like the same movies or food, and can't agree where to go on vacation. One is horny late at night, the other only in the morning. You think she is putting on too much weight, she says you drink too much. You are always putting her down about talking too much on the phone, she hates it when you spend the entire weekend watching sports. Her funny laugh embarrasses you, she complains that you are crude to her friends and tell inappropriate dirty jokes. She says you are cold just like your mother. You insist she and her family never listen to anyone and talk over any conversation you are engaged in. One cusses when having fun, the other swears when mad. Neither can stand the other swearing. It irritates the shit out of you that she always leaves her Tampax and ten feet of electrical cable on the bathroom sink, she is furious that you never clean the mirror off when you floss and that you always spit in the sink and leave it there to harden. She picks at her zits while watching TV, but can't stand you scratching your athlete's foot. She claims you never replace the empty toilet roll, you are sick of perfumed and embossed toilet paper and of finding bloody Kotex in the toilet. So what if you like country western and play the car radio louder than she likes, she makes you listen to that New Age, easy listening, minimalist crap that makes your hemorrhoids itch—besides, she is always telling you how to drive the car. It drives her nuts that you leave your toenail clippings on the carpet, you hate her doing her nails while watching a movie. You think she is stupid and can't read or follow the simplest instructions, she is sick and tired of you always forgetting things. You are fed up with her telling you that you can never say or do anything right around her family or friends, and then having to listen to her bitching all the way home. She says you snore and take all the covers, you claim she is a restless and light sleeper who pushes the covers onto you. She is always talking to you when you are trying to crap in private, then claims she is disgusted that you won't shut the bathroom door to take a pee. One farts and spits, the other doesn't. You pick your nose when you are anxious, she discusses her bowel movements and fears of cancer. It really turns you off when she starts talking about reupholstering the sofa when you are making love. She can't stand being quizzed about her past love life, to turn you on, and then having to deal with your jealousy afterwards. One snorts and swallows, the other is disgusted and adamant she isn't swallowing anything. You both work more, *read and watch TV more, are with your friends more, play tennis, golf, shop more, and sleep more. You get up early to get out of the house and work some more. You both wonder what it was you saw in each other to start with. You couldn't agree on a therapist, but after six months and $5,000 you both agree that therapy didn't do any good.*

Now, here is the key question that distinguishes long-term from short-term relationships. Under what circumstances would *all* of the above appear to be absolutely, incredibly neurotic and petty bullshit? The BAD Dudes have made a short list: You are having a near-death experience; the world is about to end. Now hang in there with us. How would our entire culture have to be rearranged so that everyone could enjoy the benefits of near-death experiences? See "Oppression And Relationships" on the following page.

Attitude Adjuster: *You want a long-term relationship — fine. Each BAD Dude gets one woman till death do you part—that's forever, for those of you not clear about the death part. You don't get to choose her; can't leave her or kill her; she stays home and raises the kids and you go to work all day long; there is very little emotional intimacy and no sex. You just survive together to the bloody end. Any questions?!*

Oppression And Relationships

Gross National Product (GNP) As the economy slows down, divorces decrease. As the economy expands, divorces increase. High growth brings women into the marketplace, creating economic competition with men. It provides women with alternatives to relationships for economic support. Hard times create cooperation. Good times accentuate self-interest. We need an economic down-turn worldwide, forever. Let's all suggest this to the Federal Reserve and the World Bank.

Social Equality (SE) Where there are clearly defined social roles and expectations for the sexes, there is less conflict at the interpersonal level. When every relationship has to be reinvented, they're unlikely to last very long. Hey! Someone has to be the man and someone the woman; someone the husband and someone the wife; and someone the father and someone the mother. It works best when the man, the husband and the father are the same person.

Supply and Demand (SD) Any significant imbalance in the supply and demand between men and women will destabilize relationships. The most destabilizing situation is an oversupply of men which leads to increased male competition. A downward force tending toward the stabilization of relationships, after age forty, is the higher mortality rate for males in later life. An oversupply of women may bring them into direct competition with men in the marketplace and increase male violence toward them. What the world really needs is fewer men and women.

Intimacy–Based Relationships (IBR) Perhaps the major factor leading to the destabilization of relationships is the relatively modern and Western expectation that they be romantically based and emotionally intimate. This expectation has, in effect, upped the ante for failure to occur. It is difficult, if not impossible, to find one person in your lifetime who could meet all your needs and expectations. This places the individual good over the good of the community (family), and makes self-esteem essential to well-being. This is a system of high reward and great psychic pain. It is also why so many relationships appear so inadequate in the face of the infinite neurotic demands placed on them.

Conspiracy Theory 1B: Conspiracy And Feminism

Course prerequisites: Intact gonadal functioning (you will be tested), passing grades in all art and physical education classes and no recent suspensions for sexual assault on campus. If you have an available elective and are trying to find an easy class to pick up babes, don't waste it on this one—take coed volleyball.

Course synopsis: This course examines the heuristical elements of the alleged conspiracy by men against women.

The Victim Model Of Relationships

This theory asserts the belief that for over 5,000 years patriarchal male institutions (i.e., BAD Dudes) supplanted Paleolithic matriarchal-goddess institutions, which has led to the oppression of 3.2 billion women in the world today and of 135 million women in the United States. It denies any biological, cultural or evolutionary forces as significant in the defining of male-female relationships. It suggests that there is a struggle for "intra-species superiority" and that "power" is the defining factor, and that men have most of it. We, of course, have no idea what they are talking about.

The "women as victims" interpretation of history denies that women play any role in their sense of victimization. It allows them to project all the blame and responsibility onto men. This theory will continue to keep women as psychological victims, and oppressed. It is commonly associated with a naive anthropology which idealizes indigenous and prehistoric cultures as somehow morally superior to modern culture. This fallopian fallacy of a better time and place is simply the latest version of the "noble savage" in harmony with the world. These are also the same women who would never go camping with you. Women would like to free themselves from any notion of cultural and historical determinism and of cultural and evolutionary forces. Naturally these silly ideas were invented by—guess who? Men. The following chart shows ways that BAD Dudes have successfully oppressed women.

The Pacification Of Women

Mall Hostages. Malls are concentration camps for women, a means of weakening their minds and spirits, keeping them pliable and dependent on men. Mall addiction keeps them out of business, politics and the world-at-large.

Old White Men. Old white men sit in their offices putting in 60-hour weeks for forty years, plotting how to keep women down. They become semicomatose— drooling, shuffling, forgetful, incontinent, sleep-disturbed, and don't know who they are at the war crime trials.

Estrogen Junkies. After women can no longer be bred for children they are tranquilized on hormones, further fostering their neuroses, hypochondria and body-image problems.

The Political Duping of Women. Women claim to have been duped but are uncertain how it happened. They have not figured out how to vote women into office after 70 years of suffrage.

Sexual Objectification. Women have been reduced to "sexual objects" in popular culture. This has left them helpless slaves to fashion, eating disorders, beauty contests, becoming cheerleaders, groupies, models and aspiring to turn letters on a TV quiz show, as the height of ambition for pre-teenage girls.

Domestic Incarceration Survivors. Women claim to have been intellectually diminished by being hooked on Gothic and Harlequin bodice-rippers, day-time soaps and women's magazines, which have sapped their minds, made them rubbery, unclear, imprecise and unable to pass that graduate course in statistics.

Conspiracy of Misinformation and Violence. Women have been kept passive by a systematic program of misogyny, threats, violence and sexual harassment. This has lead them to conclude that marriage and family are a plot to enslave them (unless they're over forty, then university researchers have frightened them with data that suggest there may not be enough men to go around)!

The Labor Theory of Conspiracy. Women claim they are forced to prostitute themselves as secretaries, nurses and teachers, seldom achieving the highest ranks of power in the society—for which men are completely to blame. No one dares suggest that perhaps men are more competent in the world in this way—it's safer to believe that we all are equal, in the same way we want to believe that life is fair.

Necromancing the Stones. Forget Sun City, fishing, the RV and that double-wide mobile. In an insidious plot against women, men die earlier than they do. This forces women to live the last ten years of their lives contemplating their kidney stones, liver spots, hip prostheses, and whether to have their hair done pink or blue.

Attitude Adjuster: *The women as victims/men as oppressors paradigm reached its most enlightened expression with the suggestion that men are not "cost-effective" and that a gender tax should be levied against us, because we are responsible for most of the violence in the world, no doubt proposed by a graduate from a Woman's Studies Program in Economics. Let's see if the BAD Dudes have got this straight—Federal and state taxes, spousal and child support payments, Domestic Incarceration Survivors reparations and now, a dick tax!*

Wait one gosh darn minute here. The small dicks are already arguing that the big dicks should be taxed more (i.e., by the inch). We, of course, think this is extremely unfair and that there should be a flat tax on all dicks, except perhaps an exemption for the really puny ones. And what about the hermaphrodites and transsexuals, and some of us think butch lesbians who use dildos should be taxed as well.

Pretty soon men will be bragging about how many taxes they paid last year. There will be arguments—you show me yours, I will show you mine, as they whip out their tax returns. The evolutionary impact of this tax is unknown. In 10,000 years an average man could have a dick .5 inch long or 1.5 foot long depending on the tax codes. Some Dudes are calling for a tax on ugly women or women who have children or big breasts and women who practice economic theory. Better yet, the BAD Dudes suggest we just drop the whole idea.

What Do Women Want?

Bio-Evolutionary Theory (BET) has finally provided a simple answer to this age-old question asked by men. A clear understanding of this answer will greatly enhance your chances with women. However, you will have to follow a complicated, tortuous path. The BAD Dudes will try to summarize the key points for you.

> **BET 1**: We all compete for valuable resources in order to survive.

Interpretation: You have go to be kidding, he who has the most toys really does win! Nope, he who has the most successful and competitive children wins.

> **BET 2**: Out of this competition, evolution utilizes natural selection to determine those characteristics that increase survivability.

Interpretation: It's not how big it is, it's how you use it. There might be a good reason you aren't scoring in double digits: It's for the good of the species—you altruist, you.

> **BET 3**: Tactics that have been most successful at attracting female mates have been carefully selected throughout evolutionary history. Desirable traits that are reproductively valuable give an advantage over male competitors in successfully mating.

Interpretation: Life is a breeding experiment by women on men. If you don't have children you aren't even in the game, unless you're one of those childless high status males monopolizing the reproductive years of many women—you rogue, you!

BET 4: Intrasexual competition is not about knife fights and gun duels. These are too dangerous even for the eventual winner. It is really about a "battle of resources," those behaviors that help you acquire "limited or better resources" at the expense of your competitor.

Interpretation: Power, status, education and money. No, we don't think we have left any-thing out.

BET 5: For men, the skills and resources they require include: (a) skill at locating mates; (b) having effective mate-attracting behaviors; and (c) acquiring resources that are highly desired by members of the opposite sex.

Interpretation: For the average guy a very expensive car is what you need here. It helps you find women, gets their attention and impresses them all at the same time.

BET 6: Males and females have different reproductive strategies in attracting mates: *Males* attempt to "maximize" copulatory opportunities. They can afford to do this because they have less invested in the outcome. *Females* develop a strategy that creates "maximum" choice, holding back until the best candidate is identified.

Interpretation: What may be a one-night stand for a man is a potential 20-year investment for a woman. Men will lie, cheat, deceive and spend beyond their means. Women have to play hard-to-get and figure out who's blowing smoke up their asses here.

BET 7: Females look for males who will provide the maximum "social, psychological, and material resources." Competition among males centers on acquiring and displaying these resources.

Interpretation: Initially it's about dueling stereo systems, Rolexes and ski weekends. Quickly it becomes about whether you can commit, a diamond engagement ring and a house with a two-car garage.

BET 8: Males seek out those characteristics in females that demonstrate powerful cues to reproductive value. These include: youth, health, physical appearance and attractiveness.

Interpretation: Men seek out attractive reproductive-age women, who not only play hard-to-get but *are* hard to get.

BET 9: Both sexes need to exhibit the following characteristics, in addition to the other BETs: empathy, kindness, good manners, helpfulness, and humor. These all indicate an ability to nurture children.

Interpretation: While being successful and beautiful is never easy, it's not enough and is almost certainly boorish.

195

So, What Do Women Want? They want alpha Dudes who are competitive, successful at their jobs, ready and able to become emotionally involved, make a long-term commitment and help care for and raise children. They want men who desire to copulate with every woman available, but choose not to in order to be with them. Oh, well! After all this angst, the bourgeoisie had it right all along. How intellectually disappointing.

And, What Do The BAD Dudes Want? No one ever seems to seriously ask us what we want—beyond the obvious wish to screw every desirable woman and impregnate as many beautiful virgins as possible during our lifetimes. And to have all the rest of the women wait on us hand and foot—just like our mothers did.

Attitude Adjuster: *Perhaps Jerry Hall (ex-wife of Mick Jagger of the Rolling Stones) had as good an answer as anyone. She said her secret for keeping Mick (or any man) from straying from a relationship is—"Even if you have only two seconds, drop everything and give him a blow job. That way he won't really want sex with anyone else." Now here is a time-tested wisdom that is hard to improve upon.*

Your Last Shot At A Relationship Should Be In The Head

By the time you are over thirty years old and meeting people over thirty, it becomes difficult to stratify the slag from the iron ore. You're floating in a primordial soup of fairly dysfunctional people, who are often angry, bitter, insecure, and distrusting. They have tarnished heroes, battered illusions, broken promises, shattered relationships, a life history of emotional betrayal and rejection— and along you come promising it will all be different. You both need to be sucking the same drug if you think a woman is going to give up her little plot of hell for you. In order to find a healthy person you must be prepared to bear the brunt of others' dysfunctionalness, and not personalize it or become enmeshed in it. Undoubtedly, due to some great improbability, you have found yourself in this uninhabitable eco-disaster.

What the hell is going on? The loss of relationship innocence always begins as the sweet and innocent adolescent longing to be loved and is inevitably crushed, like a soft aluminum beer can against the side of your head by some beefcake, with an intact brain stem, during spring break at Fort Lauderdale.

This romantic adolescent fantasy is always shafted, either earlier or later, it doesn't really matter. If it hasn't happened yet, your time is coming. Basically you have three options:

1. **Pessimism:** You make a secret and usually unconscious decision never to commit or care for anyone that much again (you are hurt and angry).

2. **Romanticism:** You endlessly search for the ideal relationship you never had but desperately want, and, we might add, which you never find (you are depressed).

3. **Realism:** You compromise, as a result of a chronic low grade resignation, and commit (you are melancholy).

You can be naive and innocent; a victim or predator; co-dependent or counter-dependent; angry, cold and bitter and always fleeing; or warm, sincere and caring and always pursuing; seductive, or hard to get; quiet and inhibited, or charming and outgoing; stoic, or needy. None of it really matters, they are all just variations on avoiding intimacy— screwing over the person you are involved with, leaving them bewildered and more distrusting than ever.

Underneath is the belief that someone can make us more whole and perfect, more complete or better, that they can ease our pain and discomfort from life, make us feel better or be happier and protect us from the inevitable contingencies of life. Maybe they just provide an extra pay check, take the garbage out, fix dinner and keep us from loneliness. And many times they do, temporarily. But then, we are not here that long anyhow—so the BAD Dudes say: "Might as well go for it, the alternative is even more unpleasant."

Attitude Adjuster: *You have devolved into what biologists call an <u>extremophile</u>: an organism adapted to unusually harsh conditions. It's 1:30 a.m. Sunday morning. You have just finished watching a 2.5 hour, subtitled, Italian comic-drama that has left you sobbing, wizened, melancholy, and forever despairing of the human condition. As you put the gun back in the draw it dawns on you: You have mutated from a cuddly, stuffed animal into a single-cell super organism. You are now a superfreak that can live in the ass of a lab rat for up to a year or speed-date for an hour and a half on a Saturday afternoon (basically the same thing). Awesome Dude!*

Final Descent Into A Relationship

If you are a Dude who has experienced all the above and more, then there are not many places left for you to explore in order to find a relationship. These are daunting places to descend into and are not for the timid, squeamish or claustrophobic. This journey will test you to the limits of your endurance, not to mention your patience. A Dude must search for the least desirable women. We know you are shaking your heads—no way. Not now, not ever will I ever be caught dead with one of the undesirable ones. It's one thing to sneak over at night occasionally—but I couldn't live with myself or with one of them in the daytime.

So, you say you want a relationship more than anything else. Then go where you have Never Gone Before or swore you would never venture. For BAD Dudes it requires *The Strategy Of The Least Desirable.*

Attitude Adjuster: *That's it, period. BAD Dudes and women have a long, arduous and lonely journey together and will only find comfort along the way if they can accept what is vital in the other, no matter how inadequate and meager the offering sometimes seems. In the face of what we are struggling with, all offers from the opposite sex will seem insufficient. To understand and accept this will mean you have found Relationship Wisdom. Don't despair. Nature has it all worked out—you get all the sex and chaos you can handle before you die and are lonelier than you ever imagined.*

WARNING!

RESTRICTED AREA
ENTER AT YOUR OWN RISK

The Strategy Of The Least Desirable

A BAD Dude must go where no dude has ever gone before, or will admit having gone, and seek only inner beauty in a woman. You must plunge below any previous personal concept of a minimum standard or expectation, you must suppress eons of primitive limbic and brain-stem activity, fight androgenation and gonadal formation, overcome centuries of cultural stereotyping and years of socialization, not to mention the ridicule of your friends. You must seek out and date the least desirable women.

These women will be too tall or too short, too thin or obese, malproportioned, have poor hygiene, scraggly hair, crooked teeth, noses that extend in awful ways from their faces, pock-marked complexions, and genitals that reek from being soaked in garlic and goat cheese. They will never have had a date. Wherever they go they will be looked at with revulsion, you will have an extremely hard time even finding one, for they seldom leave their dwelling compounds. Did we say they were ugly, too? They will be wild, wild women, the hags and crones of children's fairy tales, who will be timid and angry when you approach them.

They will attack you, at first. You will have to be patient beyond your abilities, and woo them for a very, very long time before they can ever begin to trust you. You will have to give up your fear of embarrassment and ridicule when seen in public with them, and then, only after a long, long time—they may put up with you.

Wait! What About The Nice Guys, You Ask?

The BAD Dudes could not end this book without a final word about nice guys, the most misunderstood of all BAD Dudes. We are aware of the unique plight of nice guys and want to address this serious social issue here and now. The World Health Organization (WHO) reported that 100 million acts of copulation occurred everyday between men and women in 1992. So how come it's been so long since you did the nasty? Do you just keep playing with yourself or do you have to give up being a nice guy?

The fact is, being nice doesn't guarantee anything and being a bad actor has its rewards. There are women attracted to both. You need to be able to tell the difference. You can't fake being bad, you either are or you aren't. It won't work trying to be a jerk if you aren't one already. Women will see through you for the asshole you are, for being a *poseur*. Lookit, basically if you are a "nice guy," you're getting what you deserve in terms of a relationship.

If you don't have the relationship you want, you'd better take a closer look at yourself. You may be looking for unavailable women, or have an impossibly idealized vision of women, or be interested in types of women who have no interest in you. Or you may be interested in women with whom you have no business getting involved. You may be nice—nice and seriously flawed. Who could possibly know all the possibilities, or even care? Maybe your separateness is a clue that you are not really ready for a relationship. Maybe you're not trying hard enough or you are trying too hard. Perhaps you're just unlucky.

Attitude Adjuster: *Remember, BAD Dudes gotta stick together. Besides, we can't all be hitting on the same woman at the same time—nice guys, go to the back of the pack before we kick your ass! If you're not getting any nookie and are afraid you might be a nice guy, take the gender challenge test on the next page.*

Are You Gender Challenged?

— The Highway Patrol is always stopping you for driving with two hands on the wheel, then sarcastically reminding you that the tag on your shirt is out.

— Every woman hitch-hiker you pick up turns out to be a man.

— You never pee while showering.

— You have never given the finger to a cop.

— You just duck and never say anything when your neighbor points his nail gun at your head and laughs.

— You always pull to the front pump.

— You wonder about the advisability of taking a mudbath at a spa that offers colonics.

— You like extra-soft, embossed, scented, two-ply toilet paper in decorator colors.

— Elderly Asian drivers give you the finger for driving too cautiously on the freeway.

— You have never stolen from your employer.

— You carry a coin purse and count out change in the express line.

— You find it hard to hang around lingerie displays and tell cute teenage girls that they would look good in those sexy panties they are holding.

— You have never befriended old people, hoping they will leave you a little something.

— You have called the Howard Stern Show and tossed his salad for 30 seconds of air time.

— You have never stood at a urinal and wiped snot on the chrome fixtures or tile walls.

— You have been taken to the emergency room and diagnosed with "Acute Zipper-Entrapped Penis."

— When your date tells you, "Drop and give me fifty," you can only do ten pushups.

If you checked *one* of the above items then you are—a suck-up, ass kissing, groveling, shit-eating, bottom-feeding, krill-sucking mollusk. Okay! Stop crying! You *can* be a BAD Dude.

Revelation #5: Debriefing

The BAD Dudes are aware that if you play with the questions raised by Reality long enough, you will become very confused and frustrated. You will devise even more questions, for instance, do they mean to imply that all women are the same? That there are no significant distinctions to be made between this one and that one — only neurotic musings about how this one seems prettier or that you kind of like that one more? Is it possible, you ponder, that it doesn't matter whether you are a tits or an ass man? Whether a woman is lesbian or straight, young or old, pretty or ugly, fat or thin—is it all the same? Is it all in the eye of the beholder? Is it all relative? Are these simply irrelevant distinctions that need to be outgrown, transcended, enlightened, insccurities to be worked out, or superficial manifestations of transitory and insignificant ego-states? Perhaps H.L. Mencken was right, love is "the delusion that one woman differs from another."

You are probably saying screw this New Age psychobabble, ascetic, meditating, lotus-eating, existential it's all-pointless-you-are-ultimately-alone bullshit. Shove the it's all relative, I have neurotic complexes to work out, and can have a meaningful relationship just as soon as I become a truly self-actualized person crap. You are not interested in the sound of one hand clapping. You want to know that when she screams, she is coming. You would rather be alone forever than marry an ugly, depressed, obese, manhating woman who threatens suicide every time you try to leave. On the other hand, she kind of reminds you a lot of "Mom" and makes twice your income.

Let's get basic, let's talk biology, evolution. It's eat or be eaten. Forget that nonsense about it all being random and meaningless. It's procreate or disappear forever. A guy is either in the gene-pool game or dead-pool game. Life is not a pissing contest about who has the most toys wins, or who eats the last meal lives. Rather it is about who mates the most successfully, has progeny, and that is the bottom line. This isn't self-interest only. You want and need a young, attractive, healthy woman for the good of the human race. You altruistic Bastard, you.

Toward this end, you have probably already made some compromises. So she doesn't have to be a stunning beauty. You've conceded that the only way you are getting into the genes of one of these genetic beauties is by rape, and that it won't even be a date rape. Perhaps you've come a little further, she can be a little overweight, or have a few character flaws. You're willing to put up with her embarrassing laugh and facial hair. Even her history of lesions doesn't bother you anymore. By now you have run up against life, and have probably had enough dates and unworkable relationships to know that it is too hard, you can't take much more of it, and there's really very little pleasure in pleasure. Trying to "be happy" and have fun all the time is too hard. Besides, no one will let you.

Nonetheless, you feel that you deserve more or better. Perhaps you believe that you deserve to be loved by someone, even by someone who cares about you. Maybe by someone who likes you for who you are. Someone (although you hate to admit this), who would be willing to put up with you. It's not as if you're all screwed up. You have your quirks, too, and you don't give a damn what your ex-girlfriends say, it has nothing to do with your mother. So you're not perfect. You're only human and that still doesn't seem to be enough.

You may be saying to yourself, wait one goddamn second—I have given up my ideals, compromised my standards, turned my back on pleasure, given up my sexual manifest destiny, accepted less than unconditional love, admitted to having faults and imperfections, and I have moved past cynicism into despair. And it still isn't enough!? What the hell does it take to have a relationship? We don't know. None of us has a clue or ever comes close to succeeding at a relationship. We don't even know anyone who has. Increasingly we are asking ourselves, why? It seems like a good place to start.

Good luck,

The BAD Dudes

Robert D. Reed Publishers • Order Form

Please include payment with orders. Send indicated book/s to:

Name: _____

Address:_____

City:_____ State:_____ Zip:_____

Phone:(____)_____ E-mail:_____

Book	Unit Price
Relationship Realities:	
An Emergency Survival Guide for Men	
by Gary Freitas, Ph.D.	$14.95

Enclose a copy of this order form with payment for book/s. Send it to the address below. Include shipping/handling $3.00 for first book, plus $1.00 for each additional book. California residents, add 8.5% sales tax. Discounts for large orders!

Please make checks payable to: Robert D. Reed Publishers
Total enclosed: $_____.

See our Web site for more books!

Robert D. Reed Publishers
750 La Playa St., Suite 647, San Francisco, CA 94121
Phone: 650-994-6570 • Fax: 650-994-6579
Email: 4bobreed@msn.com • www.rdrpublishers.com